The Art of
African Textiles

The Art of
African Textiles

DUNCAN CLARKE

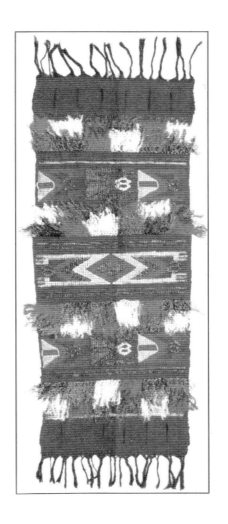

Grange
BOOKS

This edition published in 2002 by
Grange Books, an imprint of Grange Books PLC,
The Grange, Kingsnorth Industrial Estate
Hoo, nr. Rochester, Kent
ME3 9ND

Produced by PRC Publishing Ltd,
64 Brewery Road, London N7 9NT

A member of **Chrysalis** Books plc

ISBN 1 84013 518 2

Printed and bound in China

CONTENTS

Introduction **8**

Raffia Cloths of Zaire **46**

Kente, Royal Cloth of the Ashanti **64**

Bogolan, Mud-Dyed Cloth of Mali **86**

Aso Oke, Ceremonial Cloth of the Yoruba **94**

African Wax-Printed Cloths **112**

Photo Credits and Further Reading **128**

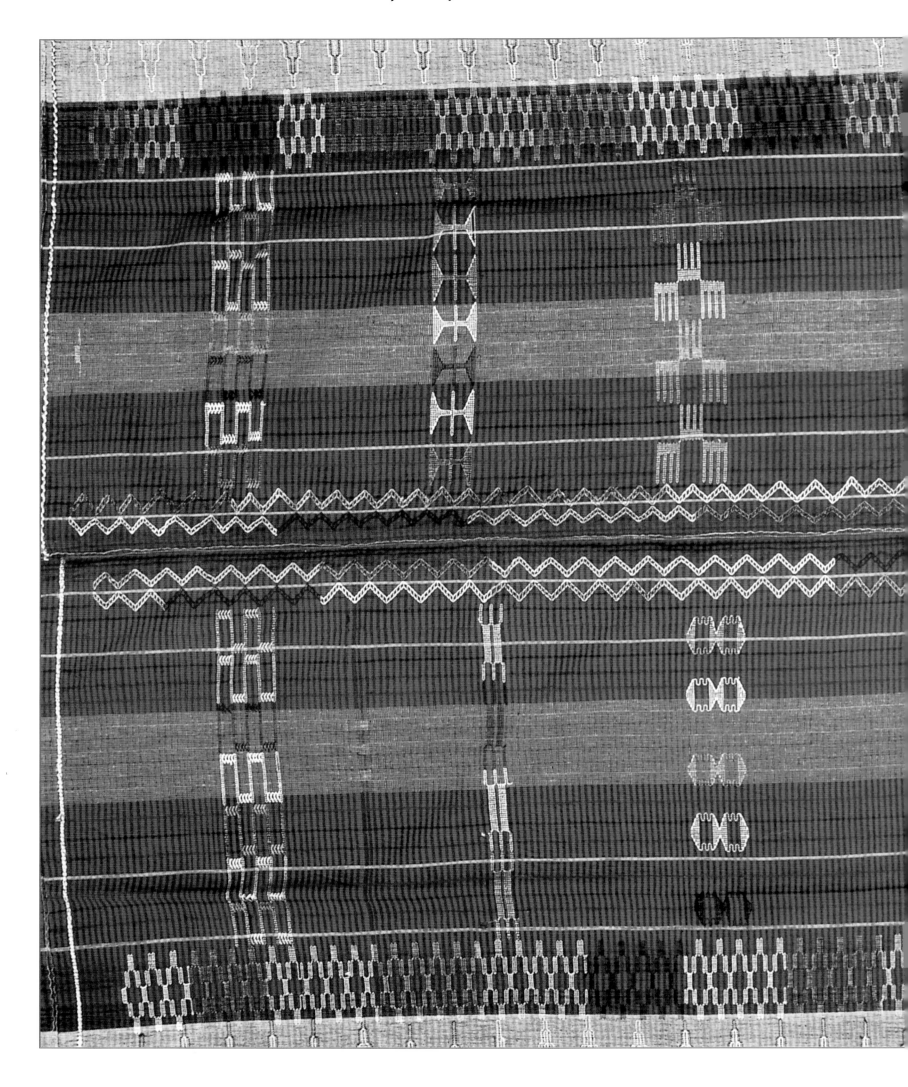

*Nupe women's cloth from Bida, Nigeria; machine-spun
cotton and rayon, 1950s/60s.*

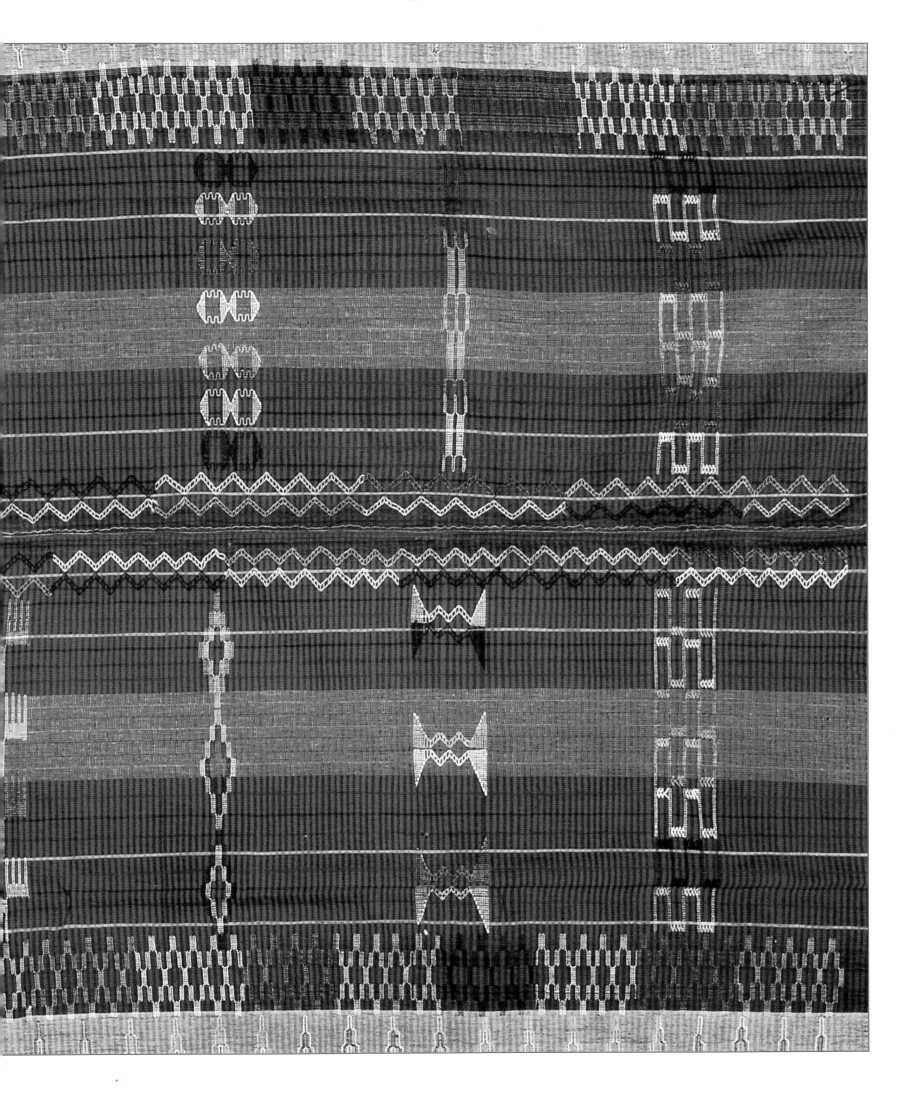

INTRODUCTION

The artistry and aesthetic sophistication of African textiles and dress has been admired and appreciated by foreign observers since the time of Greek and Roman contacts with the Pharaohs of ancient Egypt. The Portuguese navigators who first explored the West African coast in the late fifteenth century brought home finely-embroidered raffia cloths from the Kongo as prized examples of African design. Like the carpets and silks imported into Europe from Turkey and the Far East, cloths and mats from equatorial Africa sometimes adorned the houses of wealthy nobles and merchants. An anonymous Portuguese artist of the sixteenth century even chose one such mat as a suitable background to an Annunciation scene set in an elaborate classical palace. It was only over the following centuries, with the derogatory image of Africa and Africans promoted by apologists for the slave trade and colonial intervention, that misleading and insulting stereotypes of naked "savages" became the norm.

Early in the twentieth century, abstractly ornamented raffia cloths from the Kuba kingdom in the interior of Zaire were to inspire artists such as Henri Matisse and Paul Klee as part of a wider European interest in the arts of Africa and other supposedly "primitive" areas of the world. However for much of this century African textiles have been neglected even by enthusiasts for African art, and it is only very recently that overseas interest has grown, prompted to a large

ABOVE (DETAIL) AND RIGHT
Pleated dress from First Dynasty Egypt, thought to be the earliest extant garment in the world, c. 3100-2890 B.C.

degree by the re-discovery of African designs inspired by the Pan-Africanist ideology of the 1960s. In the decades since then many more Africans have migrated to the cities of western Europe and America. These new diasporas have caused a blossoming of interest in clothing styles that have developed out of ancestral traditions but embrace the fashions of the contemporary world.

This book will trace some paths through the complex and still largely unresearched history of African textile artistry. It will explore a few of the multitude of ways in which cloth has been and remains important in a selection of African societies. It will introduce some of the major forms and styles that have flourished in the twentieth century, those which are both cherished in their local context and increasingly sought after by collectors and museums worldwide. Finally the picture will be brought up to date through a consideration of the role of cloth traditions in contemporary dress and fashion design.

In addition to the raffia cloths of Zaire, we will look at Ghanaian *kente* cloths which have their roots in the unravelling of European silks to reweave elaborate royal cloths for Ashanti kings, the black and white *bogolanfini* mud cloth of Mali, the *Aso oke* narrow-strip cloth that spread from the old Yoruba empire of Oyo, and, finally, at the wax-printed fabric that dominates African dress today. Our introduction will provide an account of the main materials and techniques of African cloth production and

decoration, a glimpse of the history and mythology of textiles in Africa, and an insight into aspects of the roles of cloth in African societies. In different places at different times cloth has taken on a significance far beyond a source of functional clothing, serving as money, as medicine, as a link between generations, families, and societies, and as a key to the construction of group and individual identities.

The raw materials used in the production of cloth in Africa include bast fibres, wool, cotton, silk, raffia, and the bark of certain trees. The weaving of bast fibres, produced by allowing the stalks of plants such as jute or flax to decompose in water for a few days, would seem to have been far more widespread in the past than it has been in the twentieth century. Linen woven from bast fibres was the material used in the weaving of ancient Egypt, source of some of the oldest surviving garments in the world (see illustration on previous page). Small fragments of woven bast fibre were excavated when the treasury of elaborately ornamented brass vessels dated to the ninth century A.D. was found at Igbo Ukwu in southeastern Nigeria. Although there are some localities elsewhere in Nigeria where bast fibres were woven quite recently, the main area where it survives today, apart of course from contemporary Egyptian linen production, is in the eastern part of the island of Madagascar off the East African coast.

Wool is the major fibre used by the women weavers of the Berber peoples of North Africa, as well as by men of Arab origin weaving in the urban workshops of the region. Among the Berber of the Atlas mountains the processes of spinning and weaving are the focus of an complex web of symbolism drawing on analogies with female fertility and childrearing. The wool used for the warp (the set of threads held in tension by the loom) is taken from the slightly longer and rougher fibres of rams, while the weft threads (inserted back and forth across the warp in weaving) come from ewes. At the risk of greatly oversimplifying the extremely elaborate

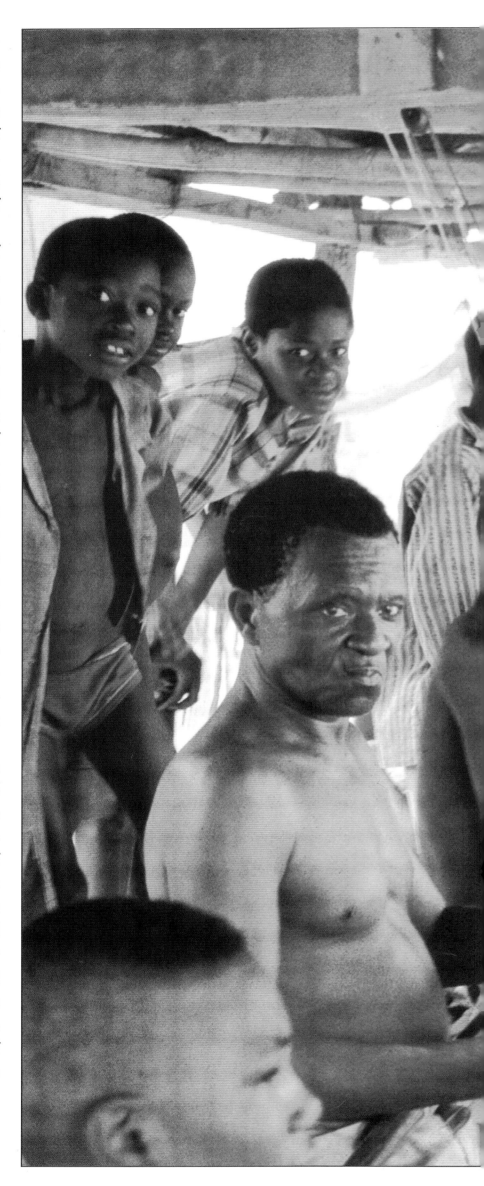

RIGHT
The Yoruba version of the West African narrow-strip loom at work in a weaver's compound in the town of Iseyin, Nigeria, 1994.

LEFT
Wool spinning in Morocco. A woman of the Ayt Brahim Berbers of the Atlas mountains spins warp yarn.

RIGHT
The single-heddle ground loom in use for the weaving of tent cloths by Berber women of the Ayt Yazza in the eastern High Atlas mountains of Morocco.

symbolism, we can note that the warp thread itself is regarded as male and is spun tightly on a spindle regarded as female, while the "female" weft is spun more loosely on a larger "male" spindle. Before the arranged set of warps is positioned on the loom, the woman raises her skirts and walks slowly over it; while the moment the mounted set of warps is drawn apart to commence weaving is a "birth" from which men are excluded. The interweaving of male warps and female wefts is analogous to intercourse, so only married women can weave. Elsewhere in Africa weaving with animal fibers is quite rare, since most types of sheep in sub-Saharan Africa do not produce wool. Weaving with sheep's wool is found only among the Fulani weavers of the inland Niger delta in Mali, in parts of Sudan, and in southern Madagascar.

Cotton has been cultivated across a wide expanse of the Sahel and savanna regions of Africa for more than a thousand years, with some of the earliest evidence for cotton textiles coming from the fifth century A.D. sites of the kingdom of Meroe in present-day Sudan. Seeds are squeezed out of the harvested cotton bolls using an iron roller and a flat stone; the fibres are bowed by plucking a small string bow to loosen them, then spun using a weighted spindle. Cotton was the mainstay of textile production in a huge region of Africa from Senegal to Nigeria, across the continent to Ethiopia. In the twentieth century a variety of colonial efforts either to sponsor the export of cotton or to support domestic textile industries have seriously reduced cotton production in many areas of Africa, as has a shift by weavers to the use of factory-produced machine-spun cotton and artificial fibres. However, in at least some areas, such as Liberia and Sierra Leone, the regular use of hand-spun cotton survives into the 1990s.

Silk is not a widely used fibre in African weaving. However, in areas where it is or was used, it often took on considerable significance. A variety of silks were spun and woven in nineteenth century Madagascar, although they have now been largely supplanted by imported fibres. The import of silk into West Africa has a long history. We have already mentioned the unravelling of imported silk cloths by Ashanti weavers in Ghana to provide the colors needed to develop the kente for the Ashanti court. In the nineteenth century large quantities of magenta-colored waste silk from the textile factories of France and Italy was shipped across the Mediterranean to Tripoli, from where it was car-ried on the long journey by camel across the Sahara to Kano in northern Nigeria. Much of it ended up hundreds of miles further south from Kano with the Yoruba weavers of Oyo and Ilorin. Known to the Yoruba as *alaari*, magenta silk was the basis for one of the three most prestigious cloths in the aso oke tradition. A second of the Yoruba prestige cloths, *sanyan*, was made from a local wild silk. This silk, which loses any lustre in the course of processing it from the web of cocoons, is produced by several varieties of Anaphe moth. Most of the silk is a pale beige color, although white thread could also be

obtained from the inner cocoons of some varieties. The silk was used by Yoruba and Nupe
weavers to weave the large robes popularised by
the ruling Fulani aristocracy following the
Islamic jihad which swept across northern
Nigeria at the beginning of the nineteenth century. These robes, often with complex silk or cotton
embroidery by Nupe, Yoruba, or Hausa specialists, became the predominant dress of kings,
chiefs, and wealthy men across a large swathe of
West Africa. In the twentieth century the impor-
tation of European waste silk has ended with the
decline of the trans-Saharan trade, and imported silks have been supplanted by rayon and
other synthetic fibres.

Raffia is produced from the younger leaves
of several species of raffia palm that grow
throughout most of the forested regions of sub-
Saharan Africa. Lengths of about five or six foot
of fibre can be sliced from the thin upper skin of
the developing leaves, dried in the sun, then split
lengthways with a comb or fingernails to produce
narrow pliable fibres. Once again, this material
would seem to have been rather more widely used
in the past than it has been in the twentieth century. In recent years it has continued to be used
in parts of West Africa, such as among the southern Igbo, throughout the Zaire basin, and in
Madagascar. Bark cloth is not strictly speaking a
textile since it is felted, rather like paper, not
woven. Bark is stripped in a single piece from the
trunk of a suitable tree, moistened with water or
steam, and then carefully hammered with a special beater. This is a highly skilled task during
which the cloth may be expanded by up to four
or five times, producing a thin but even and quite
strong cloth. The best known regions for bark
cloth production are Zaire, Uganda, Rwanda,
and Malawi, but it is known that the Ashanti of
Ghana used to manufacture bark cloth which
still has some ritual uses.

Most recent scholarship on African weaving
has classified the wide variety of looms found on
the continent into two types, based on a key feature of the way that they divide the threads in the
weaving process. All looms are basically simple
frames that hold a set of threads in tension
(called the warp threads), allowing threads from
a second set (the weft) to be interlaced across

them in a regular fashion. In order to assist in
this interlacing, most looms have a means of
dividing the warp threads so that every other
thread may be manipulated together. When this
is achieved by attaching a rod (called a heddle)
by loops to one of the groups of warp threads,
the loom is called single-heddle, while looms
where the other group of warps is lashed to a second heddle are known as double-heddle.

The single-heddle looms found in Africa
include the ground loom used for weaving tent
cloths by Berber women, a second type of vertically mounted Berber loom, the vertical loom
used mostly by women in Nigeria, various types
of vertical raffia looms used from eastern Nigeria
into Zaire, and various simple ground looms
used along the Nigeria/Cameroon border and
formerly in large areas of East Africa.

The most important double-heddle looms
include the West African treadle loom, whose
distinguishing features include the use of a
weighted dragsled to tension the warp and the
narrow-width strip cloth normally woven. On
this type of loom cloth is woven in long thin
strips, sometimes as narrow as an inch, but more
commonly about 4 to 6 inches wide, which are
then sewn together edge to edge to make the completed cloth. The eastern reach of this loom
around Lake Chad almost meets the western lim-
its of a type of double-heddle pit loom used by
the weavers of Ethiopia. Others include the
Mende tripod loom and a variety of obscure variants of the treadle loom in Sierra Leone, together with the looms introduced by Arabs to North
Africa, and by Europeans in the colonial period.
The situation in Madagascar is more complex,
with a number of other loom types, such as back-
strap looms, that share certain similarities with
the weaving technology of Indonesia.

The main method of decorating cloth
throughout Africa is the dyeing of thread or completed cloths. Although there were a small range
of locally produced plant dyes that allowed
weavers in most areas to produce a few shades of
brown, green, yellow, and in some cases red, by
far the most important dye in Africa has been

RIGHT
*An apprentice unrolls spools of machine-spun cotton
for weaving on a narrow-strip loom; Iseyin, Nigeria.*

14

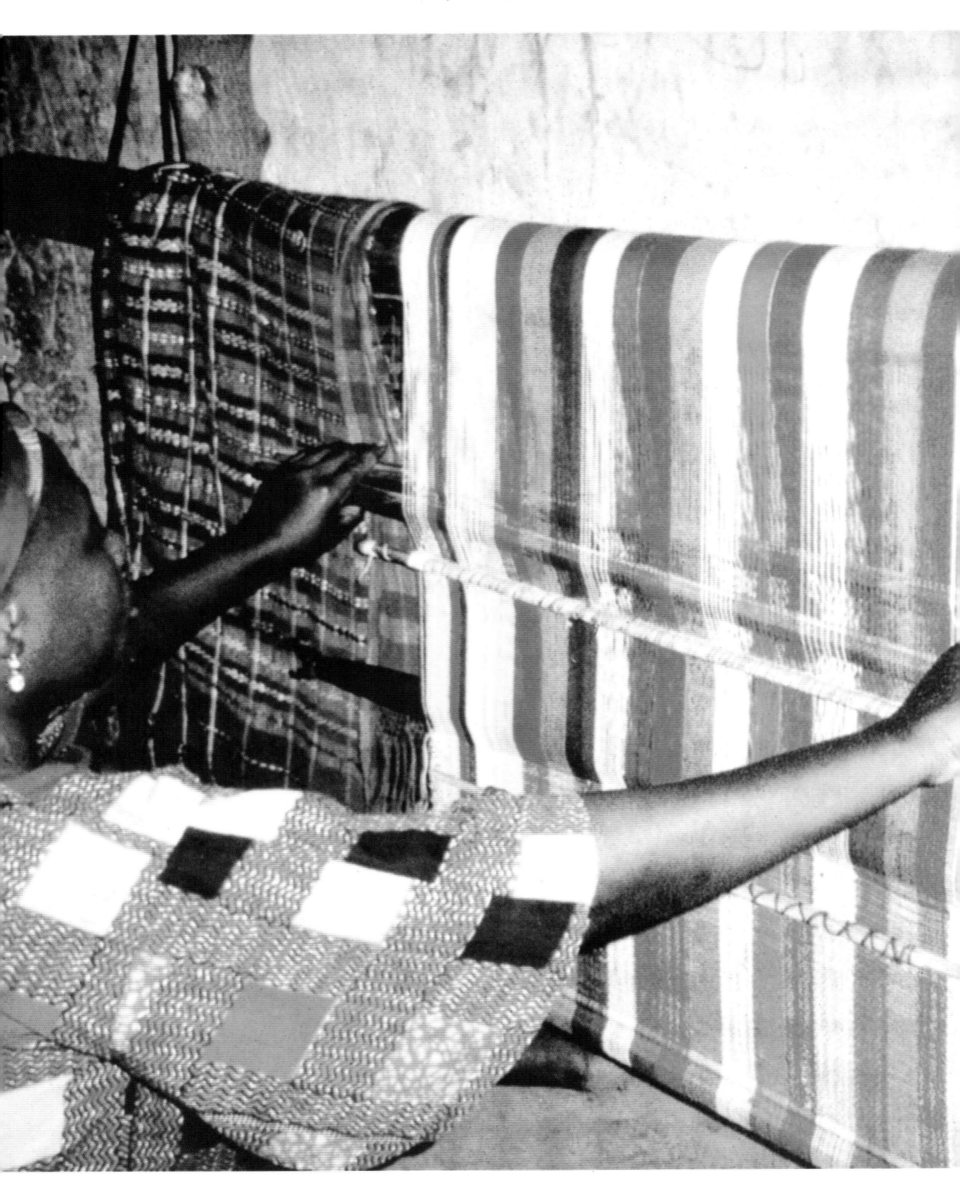

indigo. The vast majority of cloth produced on the continent over the centuries was to simple designs produced by combining the natural white of the cotton fibres with stripes of various shades of indigo blue. Dyeing was itself an important business at which a high degree of specialist skill was developed in centres such as the Hausa city of Kano. Very thin, fine quality, narrow-strip cloth dyed a dark indigo in villages near Kano, then carefully beaten with extra indigo paste by specialist cloth beaters until it takes on a glazed sheen, is still extremely expensive and highly valued: it is worn as face veils by Tuareg and other nomads throughout North Africa.

In addition to pattern effects such as stripes and checks produced by varying the colors of thread used, African weavers utilize a limited set of decorative techniques in the process of weaving cloth. These include float weaving — where extra threads float across, or more rarely down, a piece of cloth — openwork, tapestry weave, pile weave, and weft inserts. We will not go into the complexities of these here but examples of most are illustrated in the following pages. There are also a number of techniques used to decorate a cloth after it has been woven. Most of these had their origins in the indigenous weaving industry but have later been applied to the decoration of imported cloth. Dyers have utilized a variety of methods of resist dyeing, i.e. the dyeing of thread or fabric which has been treated so that part of it resists the dye, leaving a pattern on the cloth. These include *ikat* weaving among the Baule of Côte D'Ivoire and the Yoruba of Nigeria and a number of traditions that utilize starch resist or tie and dye, of which the *adire* of the Yoruba is best known. A separate and unique method of dyeing is used to produce the mud-dyed bogolan-fini from Mali. The Ashanti of Ghana utilize a

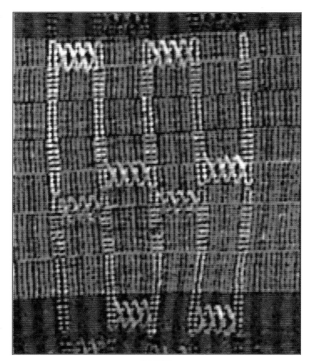

LEFT
The Nupe version of the upright single-heddle loom used by weavers in Nigeria and Cameroon; Bida, Nigeria, 1995.

ABOVE (DETAIL OF PAGE 6)
Nupe women's cloth from Bida, Nigeria; machine-spun cotton and rayon, 1950s/60s.

type of printing using stamps made from sections of calabash shell to produce a patterned cloth called *adinkra*.

Embroidery is found in numerous styles, including on the raffia cloths of Zaire and the robes of northern Nigeria. Finally there are a few distinct traditions of appliqué, where sections from different cloths are sewn together to make designs. Among the best known of these are the flags of the Fon kings of pre-colonial Danhome, and the Asafo war flags of the Fante companies of coastal Ghana.

Each of the loom forms and decorative methods introduced above have their own separate and complex histories, much of which remain unresearched. Very few textiles of any antiquity have been preserved in the unfavorable climatic conditions of most of Africa. As a consequence here we can only touch on some of the more important features of a history of African weaving.

The earliest African looms of which any knowledge survives are those recorded in the wall paintings of ancient Egyptian tombs. The fine flax fibres of early Egyptian textiles seem to have been woven on very basic ground looms, possible without using any heddle device at all. Looms depicted in Middle Kingdom tombs of c. 2000 B.C. show ground looms with a single heddle operated by two women seated on opposite sides of the warp. However, by the eighteenth Dynasty a second loom type was in use. These were vertically mounted single-heddle looms, either set against a wall or with the top beam fixed to a tree. Scholars suggest that this type of loom, which was operated by men, was introduced to the Egyptians when they were invaded by the Hyksos people in the seventeenth century B.C. The Greek scholar Herodotus described male weavers, apparently still using

this type of loom, during his visit to Egypt over a thousand years later.

Although numerous fragments of ancient textiles are known from Egypt, the picture for sub-Saharan Africa is far less clear. Spindle whorls and other evidence of weaving have been found at Meroe in the Sudan. Among the oldest textiles known are a red, green, and blue tunic and a shawl, both with what appear to be small figures embroidered on them, recently excavated from a burial site in the Republic of Niger. These cloths, which have been dated to the second half of the eighth century A.D., are from a region criss-crossed by long-distance trade routes and are perhaps a pointer to the importance of trade in the later history of African weaving.

Although some scholars have proposed a variety of external sources for the main features of sub-Saharan African weaving technology, only the Arabian origin of the East African pit loom is securely established. It seems equally if not more probable that the narrow-strip loom and some form of single-heddle loom were local inventions. In the case of the single-heddle loom,

John Picton has hypothesized that the variety of forms found along the Nigeria/Cameroon border and the apparent correspondence between the distribution patterns of the two major variants, namely the ground loom and the upright raffia loom, with the two streams of the Bantu language family point to a possible origin in that area. The antiquity of this loom type appears to be confirmed by the Igbo Ukwu cloth samples dated to the ninth century A.D. mentioned above.

By a similar logic, the area of diverse loom types in Sierra Leone may be a likely candidate for the origins of the narrow-strip treadle loom now found throughout most of West Africa. The oldest cloths associated with this loom are the large number of textile fragments dating back to the eleventh century A.D. found in burial caves along the Bandiagara cliffs in the area of Mali inhabited today by the Dogon. The great Arab traveller al-Bakri described seeing what would appear to be a narrow-strip loom in operation in the Mauretanian town of Silla in A.D. 1068. Whatever its origins, it is clear that the distribution of the skills of weaving on the narrow-strip loom, along with the tailoring and embroidery of men's robes, owes a lot to the long distance traders who criss-crossed West Africa, dealing in a huge range of goods, both locally produced and imported from across the Sahara. Many of these traders were Muslims, and the demand for appropriate and prestigious Islamic attire certainly helped to promote the spread of textile technologies. In some areas the majority of narrow-strip weavers are Muslims, although this is by no means always the case.

In most societies in pre-colonial Africa there was some scheme for the division of labor by gender, with certain tasks being deemed appropriate for women and others for men, although the precise allocation varied from place to place and sometimes changed over time. Weaving was not exempt from these ideas. Until recently all of the weaving on the double-heddle narrow-strip loom was done by men, as is weaving on the pit loom in East Africa. The picture for the single-heddle loom is more mixed. In general the upright loom of Nigeria and the Cameroon was used by women, but the raffia looms and the ground looms of Central Africa by men. It has

been suggested that men also monopolised the upright loom in Nigeria prior to the introduction of the narrow strip loom but the arguments for this are not persuasive. The gender organisation of the industry is also impacted by the relation between spinners and weavers — it is usually women who spin the thread, and in some cultures, such as in Sierra Leone, they are regarded as the owners and prime movers in cloth production, simply hiring an available weaver for a small fee to weave a cloth for them. More commonly though, weavers purchased the spun thread from their wives or daughters and so owned the finished cloth. Not least among the effects of the general move to the use of factory-produced thread has been a shifting of the balance of these gender relations involved in the production of cloth. This is important because, as we shall see, cloth in Africa is richly embedded in multiple economic, social, and religious significances.

Without doubt the most elaborate account of the religious and symbolic significance of weaving in an African society was that provided

by the Dogon sage Ogotemmeli to the celebrated and controversial French ethnographer Marcel Griaule. As part of a complex narrative that apparently related all aspects of Dogon life to cosmological symbolism, the old man explained that each stage of spinning and weaving thread was a symbolic analogy to human reproduction and resurrection — "the making of cloth symbolizes the multiplication of mankind." Underlying this imagery, however, there was a more arcane linkage between the origin of weaving and the creation of the world itself. The face of the seventh spirit ancestor became a living loom as he transmitted divine word in the form of cloth. Because of the link between weaving and the word, the processes of spinning and weaving could only be done in daylight hours. To work at night would be to weave silence and darkness into the cloth.

More common than this kind of extended cosmological analogy are myths that recount where or how the ancestors first learned to weave. The Tukolor are one of the main weaving peoples of Senegal and Gambia. Weavers in this society form one of a number of specialist craft groups that control substances that are thought to be troubling and dangerous — others include blacksmiths, leather-workers, and praise singers. The weaving group among the Tukolor, called Maabo, preserves a body of myths and weavers' lore that explains the secrets of the various looms parts, procedures to ensure effective weaving, and powers to protect the weavers from rivals. All of these are believed to have been passed on down the generations from their mythical ancestor Juntel Jibali. This ancestor, who was himself half-man, half-spirit, came across a jinni spirit weaving in the forest while he was collecting firewood. He watched for a long time, listening to all the incantations the jinni spoke as he wove. Eventually he was able to make away with the loom itself, carrying it back to his fishing village in a canoe. Juntel's mother, who was herself a spirit, then taught him how to grow and prepare the necessary cotton thread.

RIGHT
Yoruba women's dress in the 1950s, with locally woven wrappers and head-ties.

Of course not all African weavers are concerned with the world of spirits and mythical origins. For many cloth weaving is simply a craft and an occupation. This does not, however, diminish the social significance of cloth itself. Among the roles cloth has played in the past in certain African cultures is to act as a form of money. Examples of the use of cloth as money have been documented from East Africa and the Congo, but the practice was most widespread in a broad band of societies in the northern savanna belt that stretches across West Africa from Senegal to Lake Chad. In each region the width of cloth strips was normally standardized, and there would, therefore, be a regular number of such strips of a standard length needed to make a woman's wrapper cloth. This would become the unit of value, with smaller transactions payed for with one or more strips, and larger ones with a whole roll of cloth as it came from the loom. Arab chroniclers recorded cloth money of this type in use as early as the fourteenth century. Cloth was a convenient form of money because it was useful to everyone, relatively durable, easily subdivid-

ed into quite small units, and could be transported to meet the needs of the long distance traders who were vitally important to the regional economy.

Another dimension of the social significance of cloth in many African societies provides a stark contrast to the abstract economic role as money. Textiles worn regularly next to the skin, whether for everyday use, or in particular ritual contexts, take on something of the personal identity of the wearer as they absorb the secretions of the body. This close tie between cloths and their owners, a symbolic extension of the day-to-day reality of cloth use, makes them a powerful metaphorical ingredient in a variety of magico-

BELOW
Oje cloth market, in Ibadan, in the 1960s. In the foreground is adire indigo-dyed cloth; at the back hand-woven aso oke.

RIGHT
An Ebira masquerade commemorating deceased elders, 1960s. The costume combines locally woven shroud cloth with red cloth woven by the neighboring Bunu people using thread obtained by unraveling hospital blankets.

Nupe machine-spun cotton women's cloth from Bida,
Nigeria, 1950s/60s.

religious practices. A section of cloth worn regularly would often form part of the ingredients attached to a Fon bocio figure intended to act as a substitute target for any ill-fortune or malevolent forces directed against its owner. Yoruba herbalists would burn small pieces of handwoven cloth as an ingredient of amulets, while they were particularly appropriate for curing barren women or those troubled by persistent miscarriages. It is likely these remedies drew symbolic force from the significance of the cloth mothers used to carry their baby securely on their back. Among the Hausa followers of bori spirit possession cults in northern Nigeria and Niger, devotees will undergo considerable hardship to obtain the cloth necessary to construct the dress style appropriate to the particular spirit that works through them. The spirit becomes so closely linked to its clothing that a troublesome and dangerous one may be passed on to another medium by tricking an unsuspecting woman into dancing with one of the cloths.

ently contradictory impacts on issues of personal and group identity. On the one hand it contributed to the development of notions of localised group identity, as people of a particular area often dressed in a distinctive cloth design allowing them to be readily distinguished from strangers and travelers. This assisted in the formation of senses of tribal or ethnic identity in the colonial period, with textile forms among the cultural resources available for the construction of new dimensions of group identity. A conventionalised picture of "tribal" dress styles, for example, for the Yoruba, Igbo, or Ijo of Nigeria, or the Ashanti of Ghana, often developed, although usually from a considerable oversimplification of the true complexity of local textile fashions. On the other hand, however, the existence of these localised styles in the pre-colonial period was the basis for much of the long-distance trade in textiles. Cloth didn't just move from weaving areas to clothe people in regions where no cloth was produced. Equally if not more important was the

ABOVE (DETAIL) AND RIGHT
Adire cloth, starch resist indigo-dyed on imported cotton shirting, Yoruba-speaking region of Nigeria.

Although, as we have seen, many of the more simple types of African cloth were basically interchangeable, allowing them to be used as a currency, African textiles are also characterised by a wide variety of distinctive local styles and traditions, many of which were confined to the weavers of a single town or region. This localised pattern of stylistic development had two apparently

demand for different types of cloth than could be produced in the home region. In some cases this was due to economic specialization — in highly developed textile producing areas such as Kano cheaper cloth was imported for local everyday use while weavers concentrated on making higher value styles, much of which were intended for export. In other cases, particularly among the

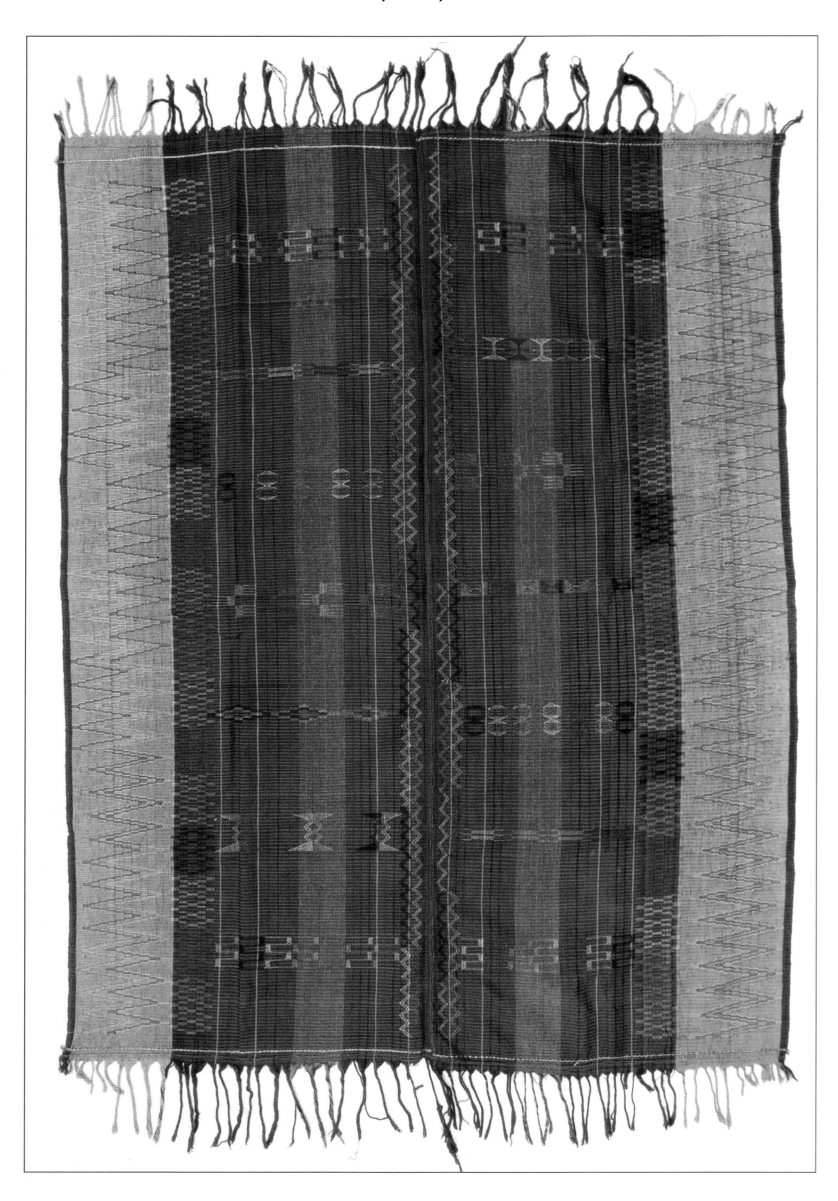

wealthy kings, chiefs, and trading communities, the motive was to enhance prestige by accumulating and displaying the sheer variety of cloths. This interest extended to both locally woven and imported cloths — since the sixteenth century Europeans had been importing a huge variety of silks, velvets, and damasks to Africa. Samuel Johnson, the pioneering Yoruba historian, records one example of such a competitive display when the Alafin, ruler of the Oyo empire, was visited by a wealthy king from the coast. In front of a thousand of Oyo's vassal kings, the visitor matched each of the Alafin's changes of robe with an equally rich robe of the same cloth. The Alafin was finally only able to outshine his visitor and sustain his royal prestige by instructing his weavers to weave a unique robe from the fibres of a silk-cotton tree.

Like many others around the world, individuals in many African communities have a love of the novel and exotic that is expressed in the collection of textiles. The Kalabari people of the Niger delta provide perhaps the best documented example of this interest in accumulating large stores of exotic textiles from around the world. Art historians such as Lisa Aronson, Joanne Eicher, and Tonye Erekosima, have explored the expression of this interest in many areas of Kalabari social practice, and its implications for the transmission of cloth design. The Kalabari people do not weave themselves, but have been trading regularly with both other African peoples and, since the sixteenth century, with European slave traders and merchant ships. These European traders brought to the Kalabari cloth from Europe, India, and elsewhere in Africa such as Ashanti textiles from the Gold Coast. Indian cloth, especially checked Madras cottons, called "George" in southern Nigeria, were particularly popular. The Kalabari developed their own unique style of cloth decoration, called *pelete bite*, making patterns on imported Indian cotton by using a razor blade to cut and draw out certain threads.

For both men and women in Kalabari society there is a series of life-cycle stages, each marked by a distinctive way of dressing on public occasions. For women in particular, the ceremonies that accompany the transition into a new status, for instance those associated with becoming a new mother, known as *iria bo*, were occasions when the family could display its wealth through the full range of appropriate cloths and jewellery. This marking of life-cycle stages through cloth culminates in the tradition of "dressing" the funeral rooms of a deceased elder. As part of an elaborate cycle of funeral commemorations spread over a week or so, three or more rooms in the deceased's house would be dressed by lining the walls and ceiling with layers of expensive cloths. A four-poster bed in the centre of each room would be adorned with carefully folded patterns created from the cloths accumulated by the family over generations. Customary rules lay down a procedure by which the deceased lies in state in these rooms through the wake-keeping period.

One consequence of this Kalabari interest in cloth has been a movement in weaving styles from one region of Nigeria to another. The Kalabari prize a type of broad cloth decorated with a weft-float design they identify as a tortoise. This cloth, woven by women on the upright single-heddle loom, is associated with the Yoruba town of Ijebu-Ode in southwestern Nigeria. In Ijebu the designs are recognised as a variety of different animals, and the cloth was mainly used as insignia of office by members of a society of elders called the Ogboni. An example of an Ijebu cloth of this type was acquired by a Scottish museum at the end of the eighteenth century, so it is clearly a tradition of considerable antiquity. However, most of the tortoise cloth owned by Kalabari families today comes not from Ijebu, but from an Igbo town several hundreds of miles away called Akwete. The women weavers of Akwete are now famous throughout Nigeria for the variety of their designs and the quality of their weaving. What appears to have happened is that in the nineteenth century the coastal lagoon trade routes linking the Kalabari with the Ijebu Yoruba were disrupted, prompting them to look elsewhere for the cloths needed. The women of Akwete then copied the designs from Ijebu cloths brought to them by the Kalabari, estab-

LEFT
*Nupe women's cloth from Bida, Nigeria;
machine-spun cotton and rayon, 1950s/60s.*

lishing in the process a new market for their own cloth.

The main use for this "tortoise" cloth among the Kalabari is in the costumes of certain types of masquerades that embody important water spirits. Masquerades are still performed in many African communities and remain an important link between present generations and the traditions of the past. Masquerades also bring together in performance many of the aspects of cloth use we have mentioned above. Depending on the context and the specifics of local traditions, they may combine both cloth as medicine and cloth as display. Egungun are spiritually powerful masquerades among the Yoruba that honor deceased ancestors, protect society against witchcraft, and act as a focus for sacrificial offerings. Yet they are also associated with particular lineages in the town, who may seek to demonstrate their wealth by the quantity and quality of the expensive cloth with which their mask is decorated. Among the Ebira of the Niger-Benue confluence, a particular type of red cloth, that used to be woven by the nearby Bunu Yoruba from threads obtained by unravelling imported hospital blankets, is highly prized as the most appropriate cloth for their ancestral masquerades. Elsewhere, for example in the puppet theatre masquerades of Malian youth associations, cloth is used simply for decoration and to conceal the performers but has no particular significance in itself.

We have introduced a few of the many roles cloth has played or continues to play in African societies. More details on some of these will be presented in the following chapters. Yet life in Africa is not all about seemingly exotic ceremonies, medicines, and masquerades. Cloth use for most people, most of the time, is an everyday matter of dress. As sociologists and anthropolo-

ABOVE (DETAIL) AND RIGHT
*Ewe men's cloth, Volta region, Ghana;
machine-spun cotton, rayon
supplementary warp and weft floats,
twentieth century.*

gists have long made clear, the apparently mundane subject of dress is itself a complex interplay of ideas about modesty and display, personal and group identity, gender roles and social ranks. Cloth is one factor among many in an aesthetics of dress that may include jewellery, scents and oils, cosmetics, hairstyles, body modification or decoration, and a wide variety of other factors. We will conclude this introduction by looking briefly at just one, often overlooked, aspect of dress in Africa that impacts upon cloth styles — fashion.

It is often wrongly asserted by commentators that fashion is an attribute only of the Western capitalist system to be contrasted, favorably or otherwise, with the supposed stability of dress styles in so-called "traditional societies." In fact the evidence would seem to suggest that at least some aspects of dress are subject to the vagaries of fashion in virtually all societies. As far as Africa is concerned, in the seventeenth century, European merchants on the Gold Coast complained that the annual changes in local taste for imported cloth were leaving them with cargoes of unsaleable merchandise to return to Europe. On the other side of the continent, importers of the glass beads that went to make the elaborate jewellery of the pastoral peoples of Kenya and South Africa found that there were changes in fashion here, too.

In the twentieth century, and particularly in the years since the 1960s when many African nations recovered their independence, the extent of African contacts with Europe and America has dramatically increased. The wide availability in urban communities over recent decades of magazines, then television, video, and most recently satellite television, coupled with easy access for the wealthy to Europe and the USA, has transformed the range of references from which local fashions are drawn. Styles propagated by the wealthy are quickly copied and dispersed among students and urban workers. In some cases these fashions are entirely based around local responses to external styles, as in the notorious "Sapeurs," self-proclaimed fashion victims of Kinshasa led by the Zairean music star Papa Wemba. More usually though, there is an influence from and an incorporation of international fashions into aspects of local dress.

The impact of these developments on African cloth goes beyond the selective adoption of new materials such as synthetic fibres and lurex. Many designers working in Africa are attempting to give their work a local appeal by utilizing traditions of weaving and textile design in contemporary dress styles. This is in turn feeding back in the form of new demands to the producers of these cloths, leading to modifications in design, and in some cases to the creative exploration of new design directions. This is particularly apparent with a growing number of designers active in the 1990s working between Paris and the capitals of Francophone Africa from Dakar and Abidjan to Niamey, including the late Chris Seydou, Xuly Bet, and Alphadi. At the same time more recognised fashion houses in Europe and America once again turn to Africa for inspiration. In 1997 alone African style has influenced the collections of Christian Dior and Ralph Lauren, while Kuba raffia cloth patterns may be found on the silk scarves commemorating the year under the "sign of Africa" declared by Hermès. While the results of some of these encounters are occasionally incongruous they are at least a further demonstration of the continued vitality of African design. African textiles are not just static traditions of the past to be preserved in museums, they remain a living and evolving contributor to brightening up the complex and often troubling reality of everyday life on the continent. The pictures that follow have been selected to show a sample of these textiles of today as well as something of the legacy of the past.

*Ewe men's cloth, Volta region, Ghana;
machine-spun cotton and rayon supplementary warp floats, twentieth century.*

Nupe women's cloth from Bida, Nigeria;
machine-spun cotton and rayon,
1950s/60s.

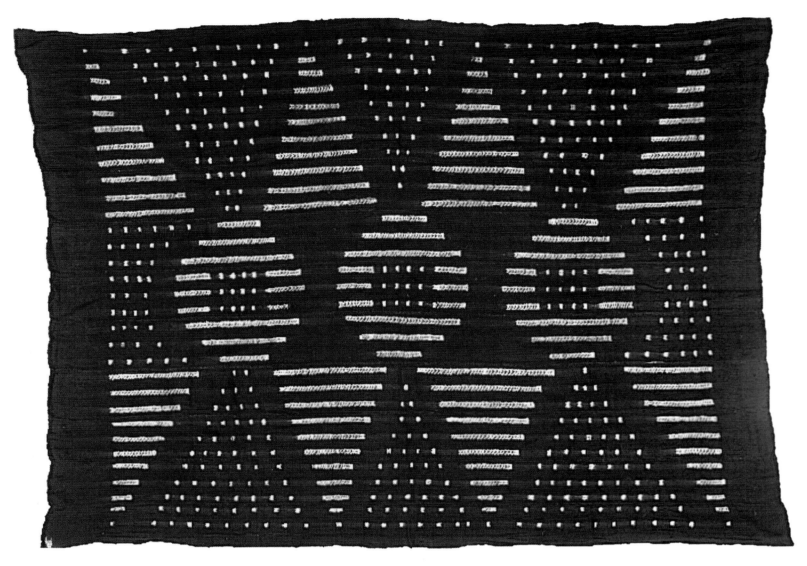

ABOVE
Resist-dyed indigo cloth, hand-spun cotton; Dyula peoples, Bobo-Dioulasso region, Burkina Faso, 1990s.

RIGHT
Fulani "khasa" blanket; hand-spun wool, Mali, 1990s.

BELOW
Commemorative cloth commissioned by wealthy Yoruba patron to mark the funeral of a senior family member. These cloths were manufactured in the United Kingdom to meet orders placed with British trading companies in Nigeria, with the earliest known example dating from the 1930s.

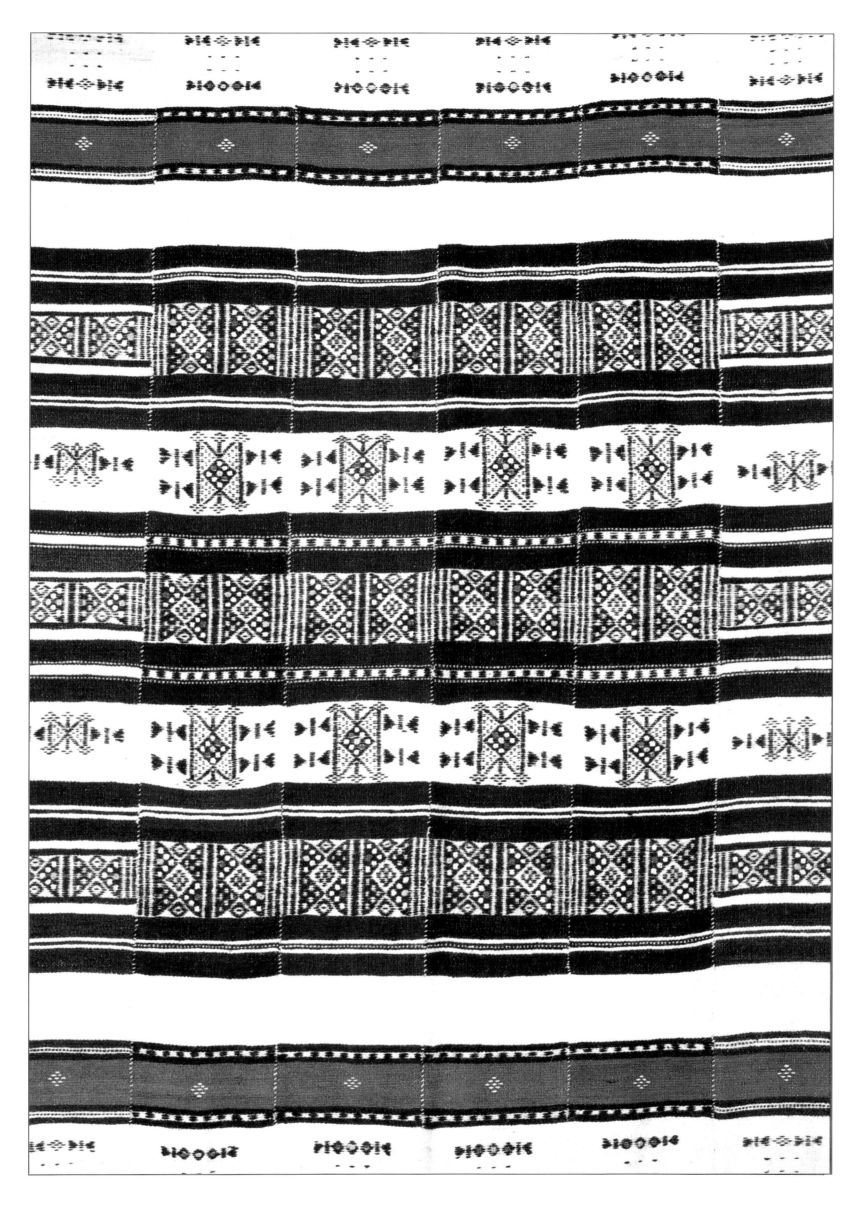

Ijebu Yoruba Aso Olona. Ijebu was the source of the "tortoise" design seen on this cloth, which has been reproduced by Igbo women weavers in Akwete in eastern Nigeria. In Ijebu a few women still weave these very bright modern versions of the cloth for use as insignia by chiefs and by members of a pan-Nigerian society called the "Reformed Ogboni Fraternity." Ijebu Ode, 1996.

ABOVE

Asafo flag of a Fante men's company; appliqué of imported cotton fabrics. The designs on these flags are proverbial allusions that promote the sponsoring company. The Union Jack indicates that the flag predates the independence of Ghana in 1957.

BELOW

Asafo flag of a Fante men's company; appliqué of imported cotton fabrics.

ABOVE
Asafo flag of a Fante men's company; appliqué of imported cotton fabrics.

BELOW
Cotton and imported silk robe of the type woven and embroidered mostly by Nupe craftsmen for the courts of the Fulani aristocracy of the Sokoto Caliphate, northern Nigeria. This example probably dates from early in the twentieth century.

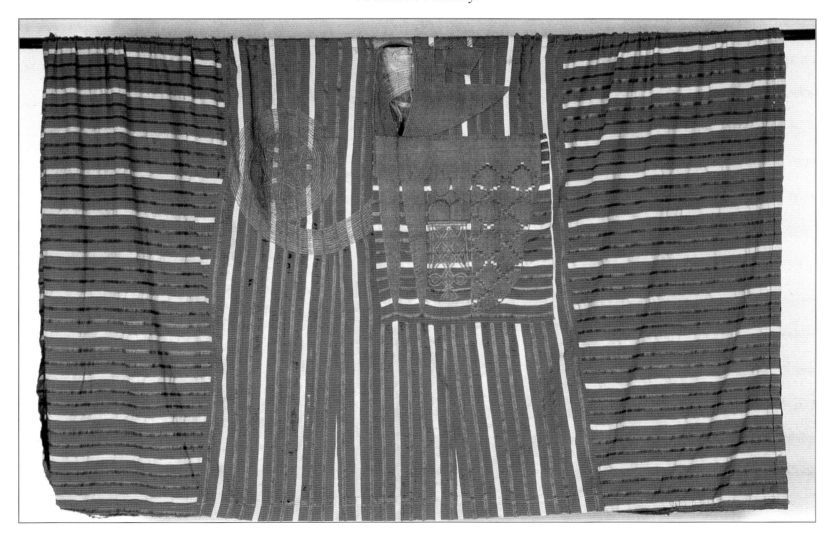

Ashanti adinkra cloth showing symbolic designs printed onto hand-woven machine-spun cotton cloth; Ntonso, Ghana, collected 1994. Much of the adinkra produced over the last fifty years has been made using factory cloth, but some hand-woven cloths are still woven and printed in Ntonso, a village of specialist craftsmen near Kumasi.

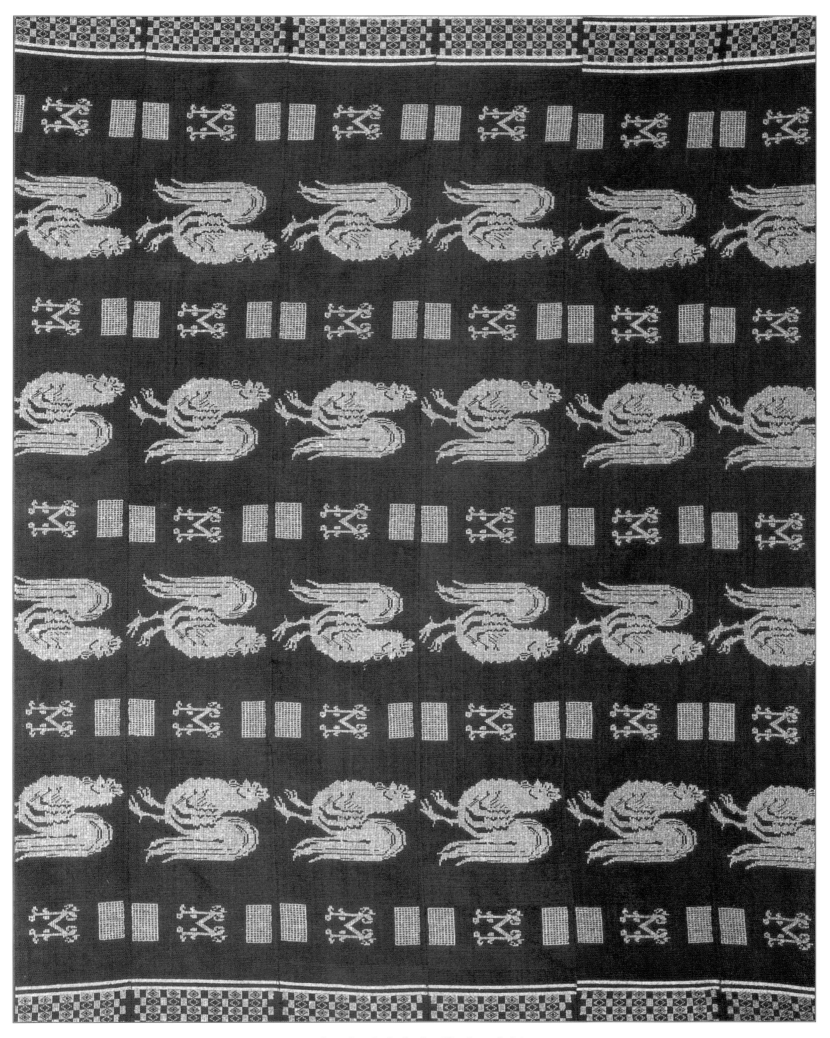

Senegalese bridal cloth. Cloths of this type are presented to a woman by her mother-in-law on the occasion of the birth of her first child. They are used by all the inhabitants of Dakar and other cities, but are mostly woven by Tukolor or Serer weavers. This is machine-spun cotton and lurex, 1970s/80s.

*Senegalese bridal cloth; machine-spun
cotton and lurex, 1990s.*

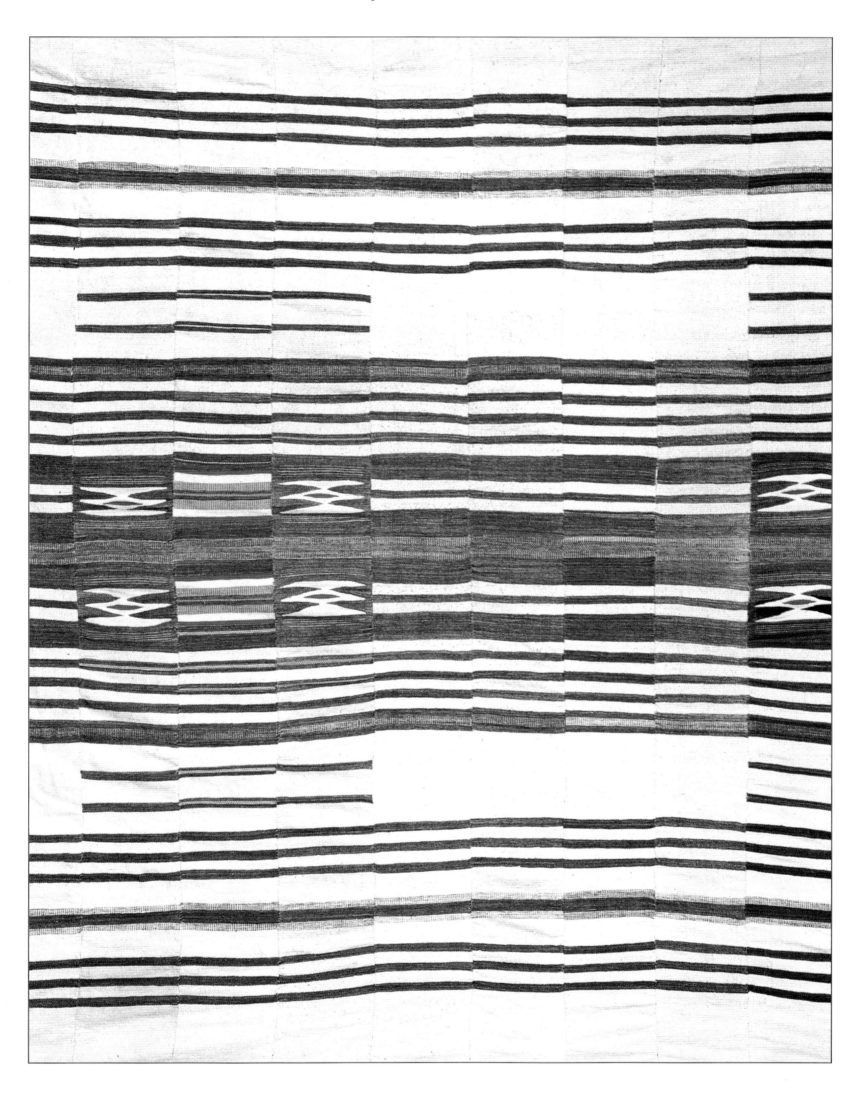

*Hausa "luru" blanket; hand-spun cotton
weft, machine-spun cotton warp, Kano
region, Nigeria, 1990s.*

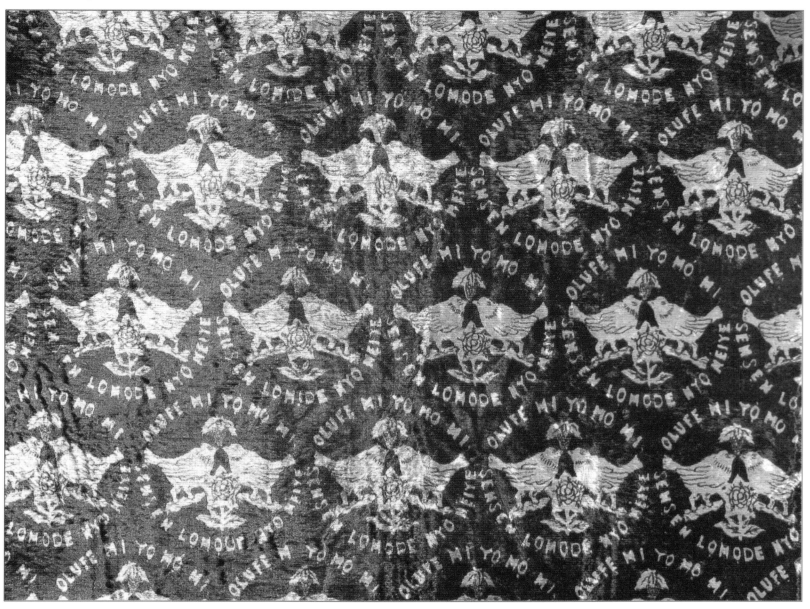

ABOVE

Commemorative cloth commissioned by wealthy Yoruba patron probably for a wedding or engagement party. The text accompanying the bird design is a Yoruba saying that translates "My love is happy with me as children are happy with birds." These cloths were manufactured in the United Kingdom to meet orders placed with British trading companies in Nigeria, with the earliest known example dating from the 1930s.

BELOW

Beaded leather skirt worn for a marriage; Iraqw people, Tanzania.

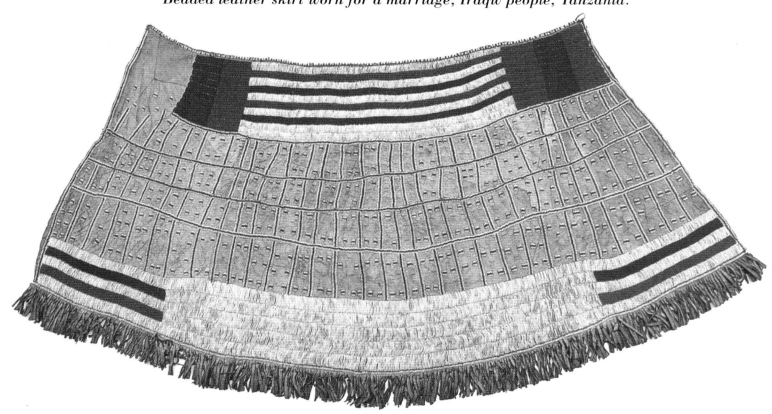

44

*Ethiopian dress of machine-spun cotton and silk, worn
with a matching shawl for church services.*

RAFFIA CLOTHS OF ZAIRE

The embroidered raffia cloths produced in the Kongo kingdom of western Zaire were greatly admired in post-Renaissance Europe and entered the curio cabinets and treasuries of nobles and kings as the finest products of African artistry alongside the celebrated ivory carvings from Benin and coastal Sierra Leone. As mentioned earlier, a sixteenth century Portuguese painting of the Annunciation depicts the Virgin and the angel kneeling on one of these embroidered raffia cloths with a typical Kongo design. Although Kongo raffia weaving died out in the face of competition from imported European cloth, elsewhere in Zaire production of raffia cloth continues to this day. The abstract patterning on cloths produced among the Kuba and neighboring peoples were a source of inspiration to European artists such as Paul Klee and Henri Matisse, the latter displaying part of his large collection on the wall of his studio. Today they continue to exert a fascination for collectors and are often depicted in the pages of glossy interior design magazines. Back in Zaire, however, their primary contemporary use is still at the funerals of wealthy elders.

ABOVE (DETAIL) AND RIGHT
Cut pile embroidered raffia panel;
Kuba kingdom, Kasai region, Zaire.

Portuguese explorers reached the coastline of what is now Zaire and Angola at the end of the fifteenth century. They rapidly established diplomatic and trade relations with the local rulers of kingdoms such as Kongo and Loango, beginning a long and often troubled history of colonisation and exploitation that only ended in the 1970s. It is a region of dense equatorial rainforests that supplies a rich variety of both cultivated and wild treecrops, including the many products of the raffia palm, *Rafia vinifera*. Early in the seventeenth century a visiting trader wrote: "of their palm trees which they keep watering and cutting every year, they make velvets, satins, taffetas, damasks, sarsenets and such like; out of the leaves, cleansed and purged, drawing long threads and even for that purpose." Cloth was woven by men on a form of the upright single-heddle loom. If the cases documented elsewhere in Zaire more recently are representative of earlier methods, the loom was normally set up with the frame tilted at an angle of forty-five degrees towards the weaver, under a small roof of palm leaves.

Although quite complex patterning could be woven into the cloth in the course of weaving, it

was far more common to produce plain fabric that was subsequently decorated by embroidery and appliqué.

Since it was not usual to tie sections of raffia fibre together, the size of the finished cloth was restricted by the length of the single fibres used for the warp and weft, giving a maximum size of about a yard square. The basic unit of plain cloth that was standard on the coast in the seventeenth century was a smaller square of about 14 inches, called a *libongo* (plural *mbongo*). The historian Phyllis Martin argues that these cloths formed a practical and versatile currency throughout the region. They could be bound together in units of four, ten, twenty, forty, or a hundred. She suggests that they were so important to trade in the region, including the growing slave trade from further south in Angola, that the Portuguese attempted to control production by stamping cloths with the royal arms.

Underlying this role as a currency was the key role that cloth played in negotiating status and authority in all aspects of local life. In the kingdom of Loango royal approval was needed before anyone could sell or buy, let alone wear, one of the more important designs of cloth, with violations of these restrictions punishable by execution. Cloth was used to display a newborn baby, to dress children at initiation, as presents to the family of a bride, as exchanges on receiving a chieftaincy title, even as payments of fines in court cases. Cloth was important at all funerals but took on an added significance with the burying of large quantities of valuable textiles to accompany the wealthy. A late eighteenth century account of the death of a chief describes how the body lay in state in a special mourning hut for a lengthy period, while each day relatives and dependents arrived bringing more and more offerings of cloth. This cloth was then wrapped around the body forming a growing bundle, the size of which was a graphic and visible demonstration of the wealth and influence of the family of the deceased. One such bundle accumulated cloths to a size of twenty feet long and fourteen feet high, so that cables had to be borrowed from European ships to help drag it to the burial site. Among the related Bwende and Sundi peoples in the nineteenth century these cloth coffins were

transformed into giant figures called *niombo*, encasing the dead chief inside a massive cloth sculpture which was carried in procession to be buried.

Although the similarities between old Kongo textile designs and the embroidered raffia cloths of the Kuba kingdom of the Kasai river valley, far in the interior of Zaire, seem marked, there is little evidence to support a direct connection going beyond a shared interest in pattern and design. Unlike the Kongo the Kuba were not troubled by European visitors before the late nineteenth century. The first outsider to reach the capital was the African-American missionary William Shephard in the 1890s. He found a society in which the Kuba king and his elaborate court headed a complex system of title holders governing a number of peoples with distinct social practices, dialects, and traditions of origin. Following other European visits, most notably that of the Hungarian ethnographer Emil Torday sponsored by the British Museum, the Kuba became noted in Europe and America for the richness and variety of their artworks.

Aside from the famous "portrait" sculptures of Kuba kings, the art of the Kuba, which ranges from textiles to furniture, pipes to drinking cups, metal weapons to basketry, is remarkable for its exploration of abstract patterning. Early visitors noted that even children practiced drawing patterns on the ground, while one of the first tasks of each new king was, reputedly, to invent a new design. The pioneering historian of Central Africa, Jan Vansina reported that when missionaries in the 1920s proudly showed off to the king and assembled people the first motorbike to reach the area, the machine itself attracted little interest but there was great excitement about the pattern left by its tire tracks!

As on the coast, the basic unit of Kuba weaving is the undecorated square of plain cloth, the *mbal*, and here too it functioned as a form of currency until it was displaced by the cowrie shell. Although the weaving of cloth is done only by men, the entire process of producing a fine

RIGHT
Cut-pile embroidered raffia panel; Kuba kingdom, Kasai region, Zaire.

decorative textile represents a series of cooperative endeavours engaging both men and women. Men are responsible for the growing, tending, and harvesting of raffia palms, as well as the weaving of the cloth, but once the cloth is complete it is the responsibility of women to prepare it for decoration. The cloth as woven is stiff and rough with loose and uneven edges. Even for everyday use it must be hemmed and softened before it can be sewn into a larger garment. If it is to form one of the main prestige garments, the dancing skirt, it will be softened by pounding it in a large wooden mortar, and in some cases treated with a wine-red or brown dye. It was previously thought that the actual process of decorating the cloths was done only by women, but recent research by Patricia Darish suggests that men are responsible for decorating the rectangular skirts that they wear themselves, while women decorate

ABOVE (DETAIL) AND LEFT
Cut-pile embroidered raffia panel;
Kuba kingdom, Kasai region, Zaire,
twentieth century.

she has accumulated sufficient woven cloth from her husband or other male relatives, she will have it hemmed and softened. She will decide on the overall style, then distribute sections of the cloth to other women in the clan section for them to embroider. For some younger workers she may outline a pattern in paste onto the cloth, but most women will be left to complete their designs within the scheme she has proposed. As the work is completed over the following months, she will collect the embroidered sections and sew them together. It may take up to a year or two before all the cloth needed for the skirt has been finished.

Appliqué, often outlined and emphasized by sewing around the design area with a darker thread, is one of the two most important decorative techniques utilised on Kuba ceremonial textiles. It has been suggested that the use of appliqué among the Kuba arose out of the need to repair the holes in cloth caused by the rigorous pounding of the woven raffia required to achieve the desired softness. Right-angled, rectangular, or circular patches are sewn over the holes that emerge in the softening process, while other patches are then sewn on undamaged areas of the cloth to balance the overall visual effect. Support for the idea that this may be the origin of the use of appliqué is provided by examining some of the oldest Kuba dance skirts in museum collections. The bulk of the patches on some of these do seem to have been motivated by the need to repair holes and achieve a balanced design, with quite large areas of cloth left plain. In later examples

smaller female dancing skirts and cut-pile embroidered panels. Among the decorative techniques that both men and women may use are certain types of embroidery, appliqué and reverse appliqué, patchwork, dyeing, and tie-dyeing. Women's dance skirts are up to nine yards in length, being wound several times around the body and folded down over a belt. The men's skirts are significantly longer and normally have distinct borders, often with a fringe of raffia bobbles. Most Kuba groups are matrilineal and it is generally the elderly woman who heads a clan section who will take responsibility for the organisation of a new women's dance skirt. When there is a tendency to cover the whole surface of the cloth with appliqué, often including some figurative designs. It is possible that these later styles, especially the figurative patterns, are a response to outside interest in Kuba art and the impact of missionaries.

Unlike appliqué, which was done by both men and women, the most laborious and prestigious type of cloth decoration, cut-pile embroidery, is a technique only utilised by women. The raffia thread is prepared by the use of local plant dyes, which produce shades of red, blue, black, and yellow. A needle is used to insert a strand of raffia into the plain square of cloth in such a way that it goes under a crossover between a single warp and weft thread, then is drawn up again until the end of the strand on the cloth surface is only one or two millimetres long. Using a small very sharp knife the strand is cut equally close to the cloth leaving two very short tufts. There is no knot, it is simply the tightness of the weave that holds the stitch in place. The process is repeated again and again until a linear block of the same color has been completed. By rubbing over the tufts with the edge of a knife the ends are split and fluffed out so that the ground cloth is completely concealed by the pile. It takes about a month of regular work for a woman to complete a small square of embroidery using this

ABOVE (DETAIL) AND RIGHT
Cut-pile embroidered raffia panel; Kuba kingdom, Kasai region, Zaire.

technique. Except with novices, the design to be embroidered is worked out as she proceeds, usually elaborating a combination of familiar existing designs, without any overall plan being laid out on the cloth in advance. There is a certain amount of regional variation in the design and color combinations utilised by Kuba women and although the picture is confused by the impact of artists from all groups working for the royal court, experts can recognise in which of the various sub-groups some of the cloths were produced.

The patterns used by women in the embroidery of cut-pile cloth are generally drawn from a huge repertoire of known patterns, at least two hundred of which are identified by name. The same patterns are used on other Kuba art forms, including wood sculpture, metal-working, mat-making, and women's body scarification. Although the regular interlacing of warp and weft on the background cloth might seem to promote a regular and symmetrical design, in fact Kuba artists seem to favor a more improvisational, fluid effect that plays with deliberate asymmetries and pattern variation. This trait, which is quite widespread in African textile design, has been compared with the emphasis on the off-beat in African music, suggesting a more general aes-

ABOVE (DETAIL) AND RIGHT
Cut-pile embroidered raffia panel; Kuba kingdom, Kasai region, Zaire.

thetic preference. Among the Kuba the love of pattern has led to the exploitation of a high percentage of the possibilities existing within the technical and aesthetic constraints of the medium, restricted only by the avoidance, in embroidery at least, of curved designs. Although many of the designs are named after perceived visual similarities, for instance to the design on a crocodile's back, others are called after the woman who first embroidered them. Anyone who can produce a design that is recognised as new, rather than simply a variation or even a faulty reproduction of a familiar one, is highly regarded and her achievement will be acknowledged and remembered whenever the design is used in the future.

The main ceremonial occasions and court rituals, for which dance skirts and other Kuba textile arts were produced, are quite rare events today. The continued survival of the techniques in an age where most Kuba people wear factory-produced cloth for everyday dress is mainly due to the importance of embroidered and appliquéd cloth in funeral celebrations. Unlike the emphasis on the sheer *quantity* of cloth evident in the accounts of funerals on the coast we described earlier, among the Kuba prestige is achieved by the *quality* of the cloths in which the corpse is displayed and buried. The matrilineage section to which the deceased belongs holds several meetings at which will be discussed precisely which of the stock of cloths owned in common

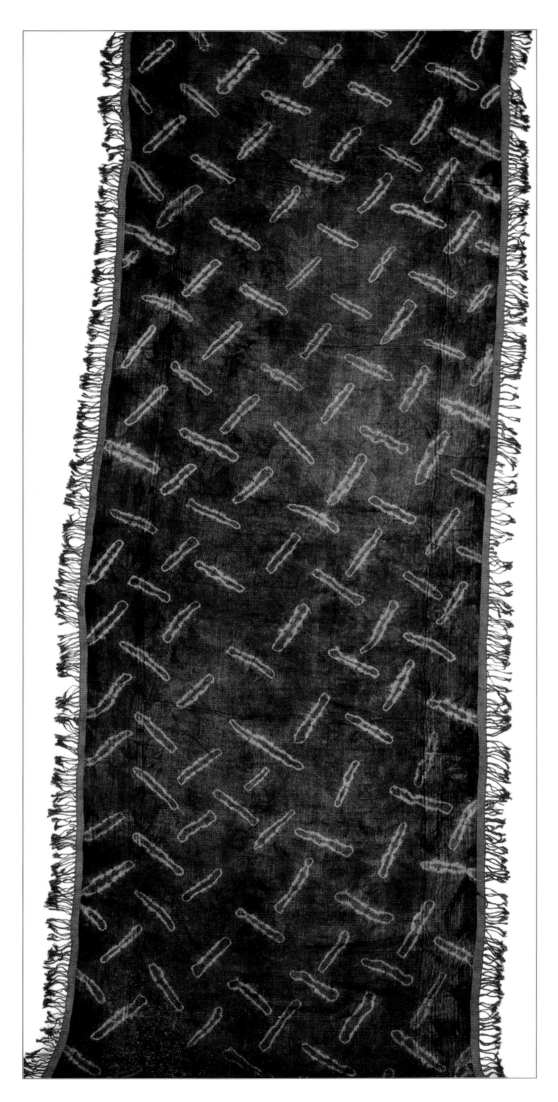

ABOVE AND RIGHT
Detail of men's resist-dyed raffia dance skirt; Kuba kingdom, Kasai region, Zaire.

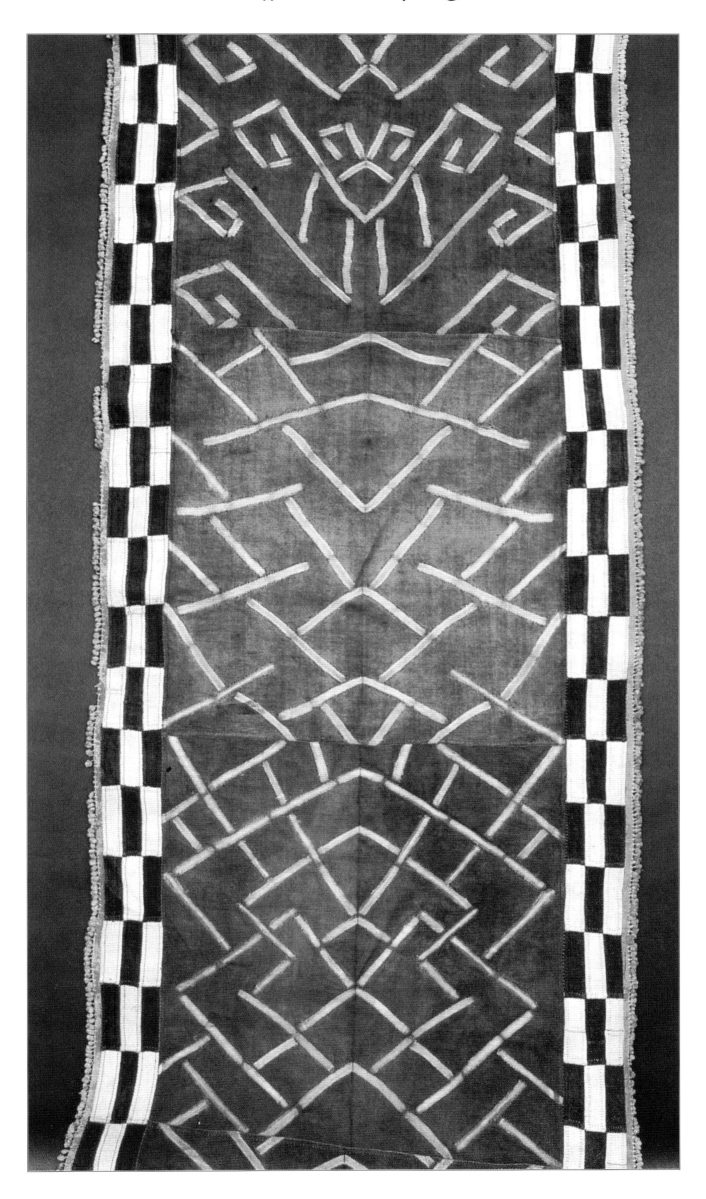

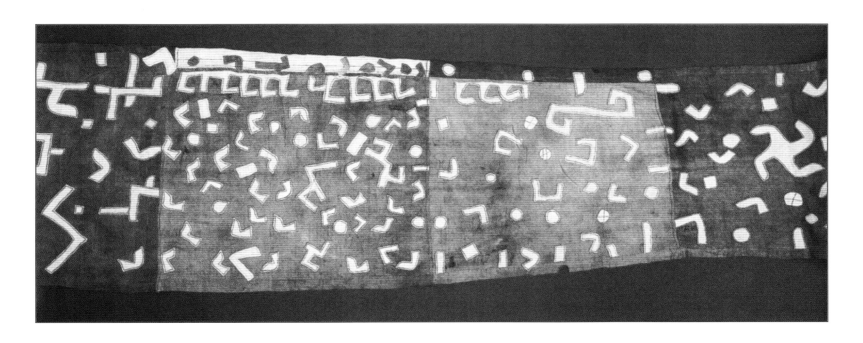

will be used. The deceased is also likely to have tried to accumulate particularly fine old textiles for use at his or her own funeral. The matrilineage of the deceased's husband or wife is also expected to contribute, and serious attention will be given by both parties to the quality and quantity of cloths that they donate. Kuba apparently believe that they will not be recognised by their clan ancestors in the land of the dead unless they are correctly dressed in raffia textiles.

The continued salience of these beliefs despite the impact of Christianity in the region would seem to hold out good prospects for the future development of textile arts among the Kuba. The remoteness and isolation of the region and the general instability of the country has prevented large numbers of foreigners visiting the region, although for several decades cloths have been produced specifically for sale through the missions or to the occasional visiting dealer. Although some of these lack the attention to detail and the improvisational design that characterises the best of Kuba textile artistry, they at least make available to a wider world an inspiring glimpse of an extraordinarily creative design tradition.

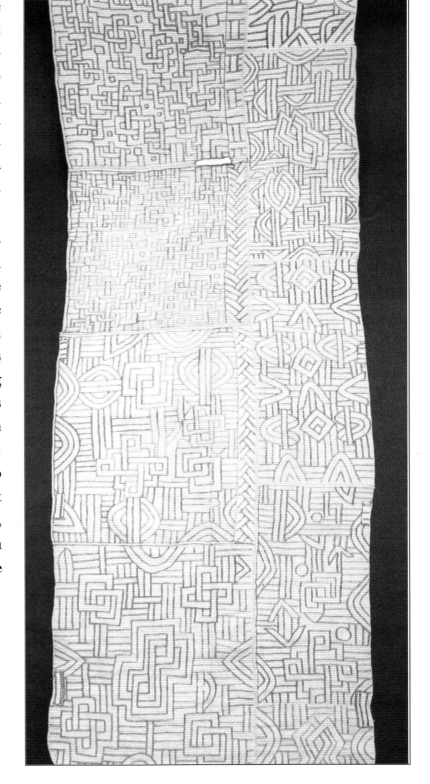

LEFT, TOP AND RIGHT
*Detail of men's raffia appliqué dance skirt;
Kuba kingdom, Kasai region, Zaire.*

ABOVE AND LEFT
Detail of men's raffia appliqué dance skirts; Ngongo,
Kuba kingdom, Kasai region, Zaire.

KENTE, ROYAL CLOTH OF THE ASHANTI

The cloths woven in the nineteenth century for the court of the Asantehene, the king of the Ashanti empire which extended over much of the present-day state of Ghana, were probably the ultimate achievement of the West African narrow-strip weavers' art. The raw material for this artistry came from Europe in the form of silk fabrics that were carefully unpicked to obtain thread which could then be re-woven into narrow-strip cloth on looms that utilised two, and in some cases even three, sets of heddles to multiply the complexity of ornamental design. The king's weavers were and still are grouped in a village called Bonwire near the Ashanti capital of Kumasi, part of a network of villages housing other craft specialists including goldsmiths, the royal umbrella makers, stool carvers, adinkra dyers, and blacksmiths. Although the high-point of the Ashanti royal weavers' artistry seems to have passed with the conquest of the kingdom by the British at the end of the century, and its subsequent incorporation into the Gold Coast Colony and later the state of Ghana, kente cloth remains an important contributor to African dress today. Recognised worldwide, it has taken on a new role as a symbolic affirmation of African identity and Pan-African unity that has struck a particular

ABOVE
The spokesman of Omanhene of Akrokerri, one of the senior regional rulers of the Ashanti Empire.

RIGHT
An Ashanti weaver at Bonwire, the village of specialist weavers for the royal court at Kumasi, Ghana, 1994.

chord with African-Americans and exiled Africans everywhere.

The Ashanti empire arose in the seventeenth century under the leadership of the first Asantehene, Osei Tutu, with an expanding kingdom based around the capital of Kumasi deep in the forest zone. It is likely that bark cloth rather than woven textiles had formed the mainstay of local dress over previous centuries, with weaving introduced from the cotton growing areas of the savanna belt further north. Bark cloth subsequently became regarded as the dress of poor people and slaves, but is still worn by the king at one stage of the annual Odwira yam festival. An Ashanti weavers' origin myth recalls that the first weaver, Otah Kraban, brought a loom back to Bonwire after a journey to the Bondoukou region of Côte d'Ivoire. An alternative legend recalls that, during the reign of Osei Tutu, the first weaver learnt his skill by studying the way in which a spider spun its web. The spider, Anansi, is an important figure symbolising trickery and wisdom in Ashanti folklore. Away from the court, cotton weaving supplied much of the everyday dress for the Ashanti people, in the form of striped patterned cloths, mostly of indigo blue and white, until it was largely displaced

by wax prints and other imported textiles in the present century.

Although silk weaving would seem to have evolved locally out of the older practice of cotton cloth production, many decades of practice and experimentation would have been needed to achieve the level of complexity and technical sophistication noted in court weavers from the eighteenth century onwards. Unfortunately very few cloths that may be dated to the early decades of Ashanti court weaving have been preserved, so it is no longer possible to document the stages of stylistic development, although it is likely that textiles imported into Ashanti from the north were as important an influence as the European cloths that supplied the raw materials, which were brought up from the coast. Cloths, including woolen blankets woven by the Fulani people, are still highly prized in Ghana today.

One of the first accounts of Ashanti royal silk weaving comes from the 1730s when a man sent to the court of King Opokuware by a Danish trader observed that the king "brought silk taffeta and materials of all colors. The artist unraveled them . . . woolen and silk threads which they mixed with their cotton and got many colors." Silk was also imported into Ashanti from south-

ern Europe via the trans-Saharan caravan trade. Many kente cloths, including most probably the earlier ones, utilised silk for a range of decorative techniques on a background of warp-striped cotton cloth, but some of the finest cloths prepared for use by royalty and chieftains were woven wholly from silk.

The Ashanti court, based at Kumasi, was undoubtedly amongst the wealthiest and most elaborate in Africa. Some idea of its splendor may be gained from this excerpt from the first impressions recorded by T.E. Bowdich, an English visitor to Kumasi in 1817, in his book *Mission from Cape Coast to Ashantee*: "an area nearly a mile in circumference was crowded with magnificence and novelty . . . The sun was reflected, with a glare scarcely more supportable than the heat, from the massy gold ornaments, which glistened in every direction . . . At least a hundred large umbrellas, or canopies, which could shelter thirty persons, were sprung up and down by the bearers with brilliant effect. The caboceers, as did their superior captains and attendants, wore Ashantee cloths of extravagant price . . . They were of incredible size and weight, and thrown over the shoulder exactly like a Roman toga; a small silk fillet generally

LEFT
The two pairs of heddles used to produce the alternation of warp and weft-faced sections that is characteristic of Ashanti kente cloth; Bonwire, 1994.

RIGHT
A men's silk cloth with alternating sections of warp and weft-faced plain weave and supplementary weft float decoration; twentieth century, Ashanti.

encircled their temples, and massy gold neck-laces intricately wrought, suspended Moorish charms . . ." Although the wealth and temporal power of the Asantehene are much reduced today, the Ashanti court is still capable of mount-ing similar elaborate and spectacular ceremonial displays on important occasions such as annual festivals and anniversaries. In August 1995 an estimated 70,000 guests attended festivities to mark the 25th anniversary of the coronation of the present King Asantehene Opuku Ware II. Other kings rule in similar style over subsidiary kingdoms, replicating the regalia and rankings of the central court on a smaller scale. From the earliest times court regalia, including the rights to own and wear certain cloths, have been active-ly used to promote and cement the cultural unity of the diverse populations brought under Ashanti control.

In many kente cloths the design effect is achieved by alternating regularly positioned blocks of pattern in bright-colored silk with the more muted colors of the warp-striped plain weave background. Interestingly it is the back-ground designs, the configurations of warp

stripes of varying widths, that provide the basis for most pattern names. As might be expected in a culture so interested in proverbs and verbal wordplay, there is a large vocabulary of pattern names still remembered by elderly weavers. Some of these names, such as Atta Birago and Afua Kobi, refer to the individuals, in these cases two Queen Mothers, for whom the designs were first woven. Others refer to historical inci-dents, to household objects, to proverbs, or to certain circumstances of the cloth's use. For instance Rattray recorded in 1927 that a design known as *Nyawoho* (he has become rich), was supposed to be worn only by men who had more than a thousand pounds worth of gold dust. More recently designs have been developed that were named after prominent figures in indepen-dent Ghana, such as Fathia Nkrumah, the Egyptian wife of the first President.

The most commonly seen designs are pro-duced by combining two distinct decorative tech-niques. The first, supplementary weft float, involves the addition of extra weft threads that do not form part of the basic structure of the cloth. Instead they float across sections of the

LEFT (DETAIL) AND RIGHT
Kente, adinkra, wax prints, and a woolen cloth imported from the Niger bend region of Mali, form part of the rich display of the court attendants of the Omanhene of Akrokerri during the celebration of the Yam festival in 1964.

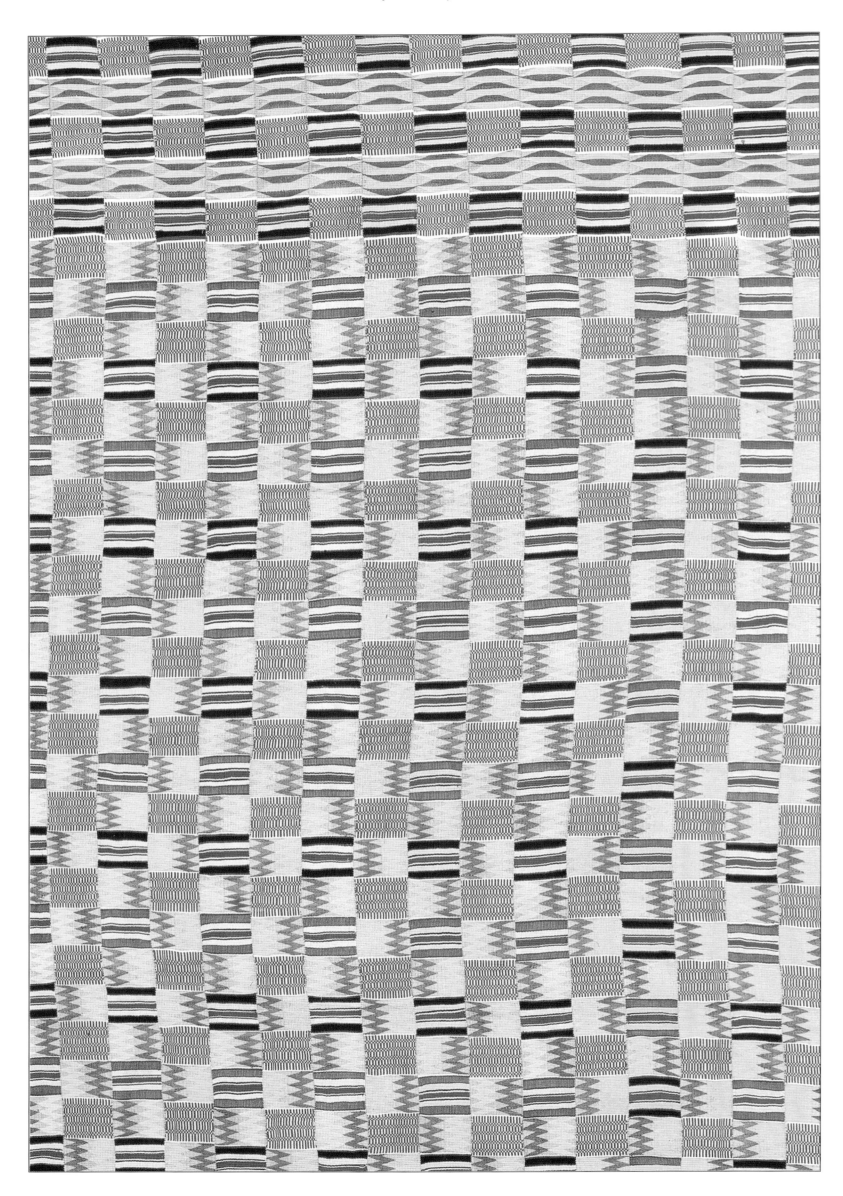

ground weave, appearing on one face of the cloth over maybe six or eight warp then crossing through the warp to the back, floating there, then returning again to the top face. Rows of these wefts are arranged to form designs such as triangles, wedges, hour-glass shapes etc. The second effect is to create solid blocks of colored thread across the cloth strip entirely concealing the warp. Without dwelling too much on the technicalities, this effect is achieved by the use of a technical innovation unique to the weaving of southern Ghana, namely the use of a second set of heddles that has the effect of bunching together groups of warp threads allowing them to be hidden by the weft. The design of most kente cloths involves framing areas of weft float decoration within the narrow solid bands called *bankuo*. The finest and most elaborate examples of this style and perhaps the most spectacular cloths ever woven in Africa, completely covered the underlying warp design with alternating sections exploiting the full range of weft float designs between very narrow bands, producing a cloth named Adwinasa, meaning "fullness of ornament."

Certain cloths, of a style called asasia, pushed the technical complexity even further, although perhaps without surpassing the design virtuosity, by using a third set of heddles.

Without a lengthy technical explanation it is hard to explain the significance of this, but its effect was to allow weft float inlay patterns to be set at sharper angle. This distinguished the resulting cloths in a way apparent to connoisseurs at the height of the Ashanti empire but is a level of refinement no longer needed today. Only the king himself could authorise the weaving of asasia cloths and the right to wear one was a highly prized honour granted as a reward to particularly loyal chiefs. It is thought that the skill of weaving these cloths has been lost, although no doubt it could be done if the demand were still there.

Although the Ashanti continued to wear kente in the context of court ceremonial and other important occasions throughout the twentieth century, the present wider popularity of the cloth owes much to political developments in the early independence era. Ghana was the first of the African states to achieve independence in 1957, and its first President, Kwame Nkrumah, became a major figure on the world stage. He adopted the wearing of kente and other locally woven cloths as a visual symbol of his commitment to cultural nationalism and Pan-African unity. Although the optimistic hopes of this period soon faded, and Nkrumah himself was overthrown in a coup, the new significance imparted

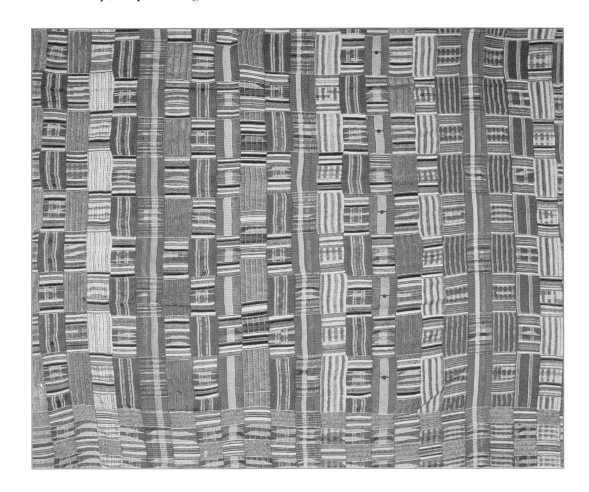

FAR LEFT AND LEFT
A men's silk cloth with alternating sections of warp and weft-faced plain weave and supplementary weft float decoration; twentieth century, Ashanti.

A men's silk cloth with alternating sections of warp and weft-faced plain weave and supplementary weft float decoration; twentieth century, Ashanti.

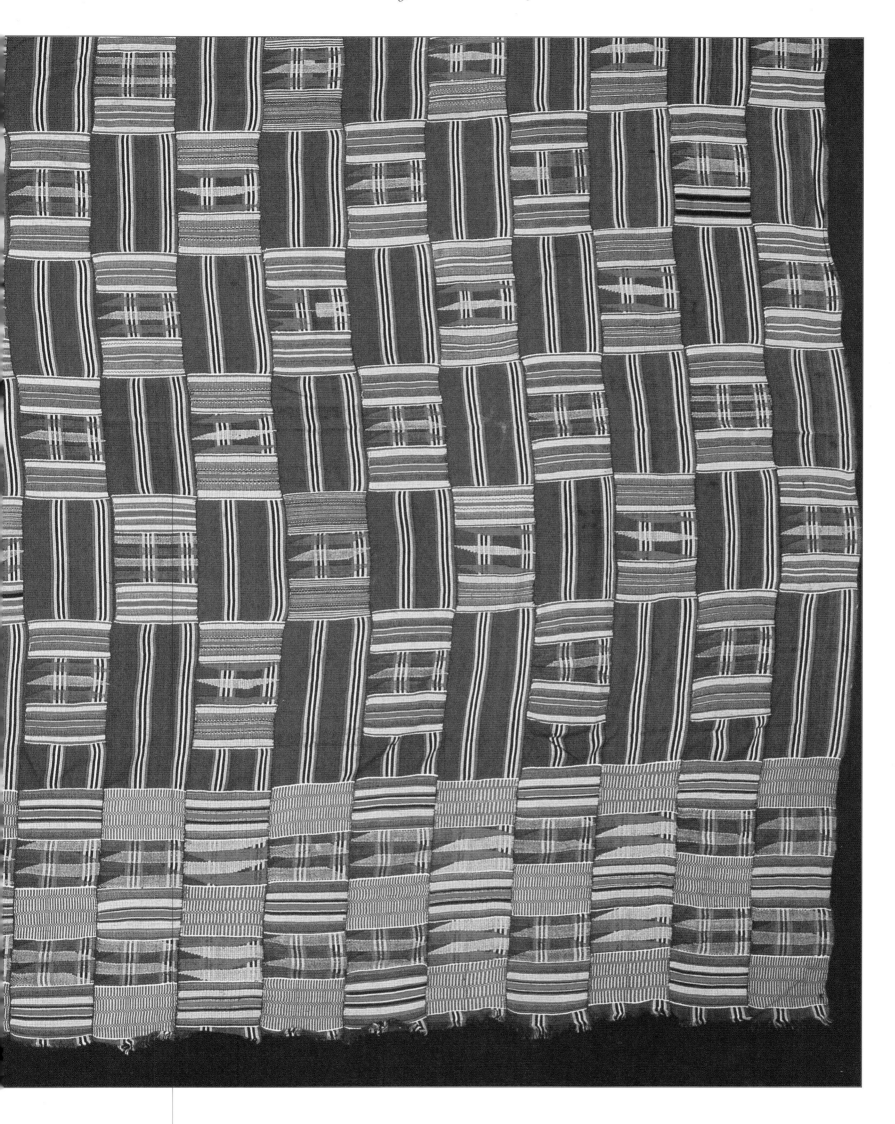

to kente at this time lives on. Within Ghana kente and other local cloths remain the prestige dress of political leaders, notably in the campaign pictures of President Rawlings' Ashanti opponent during the 1996 election. Rawlings himself is not an Ashanti but is often pictured wearing kente for official portraits. Away from Africa, kente is seen as the predominant African design, with large quantities of often low-quality cotton and imitation silk cloths exported from Ghana for use in a variety of garments from waistcoats to baseball caps, while factories in Ghana and throughout West Africa reproduce simplified kente designs on cheaper wax-printed fabrics.

Although Ashanti weavers supply much of this new demand for kente cloth, a considerable proportion is produced by weavers from the neighboring Ewe peoples. The Ewe are believed to have arrived at their present location around the Volta delta in the seventeenth century after a series of migrations from the east. Unlike the Ashanti they were never a unified political entity with a powerful court, being ruled instead by numerous village chiefs and shrine priests. Perhaps as a consequence of this lack of a centralised authority imposing common standards, Ewe weaving is far more diverse than that of the Ashanti. Although they did supply important regalia to local chiefs, Ewe weavers worked primarily for sale through markets. Today Ewe weavers are concentrated around two towns, Kpetoe and Agbozume, with the latter the site of a large cloth market which draws buyers from throughout Ghana as well as neighboring countries.

Ewe weavers utilize an almost identical form of the narrow-strip loom to that of the Ashanti, and there is considerable evidence to suggest mutual influence between the weavers of the two traditions, as might be expected from the long history of contacts, both through trade and conquest, between their peoples. However Ewe weaving has also been influenced by and exercized an influ-

RIGHT
Ewe weaving in the 1990s. Detail of a men's cloth with supplementary weft float designs over a background of supplementary warp float weave; cotton, rayon, and lurex, from the Volta region of Ghana.

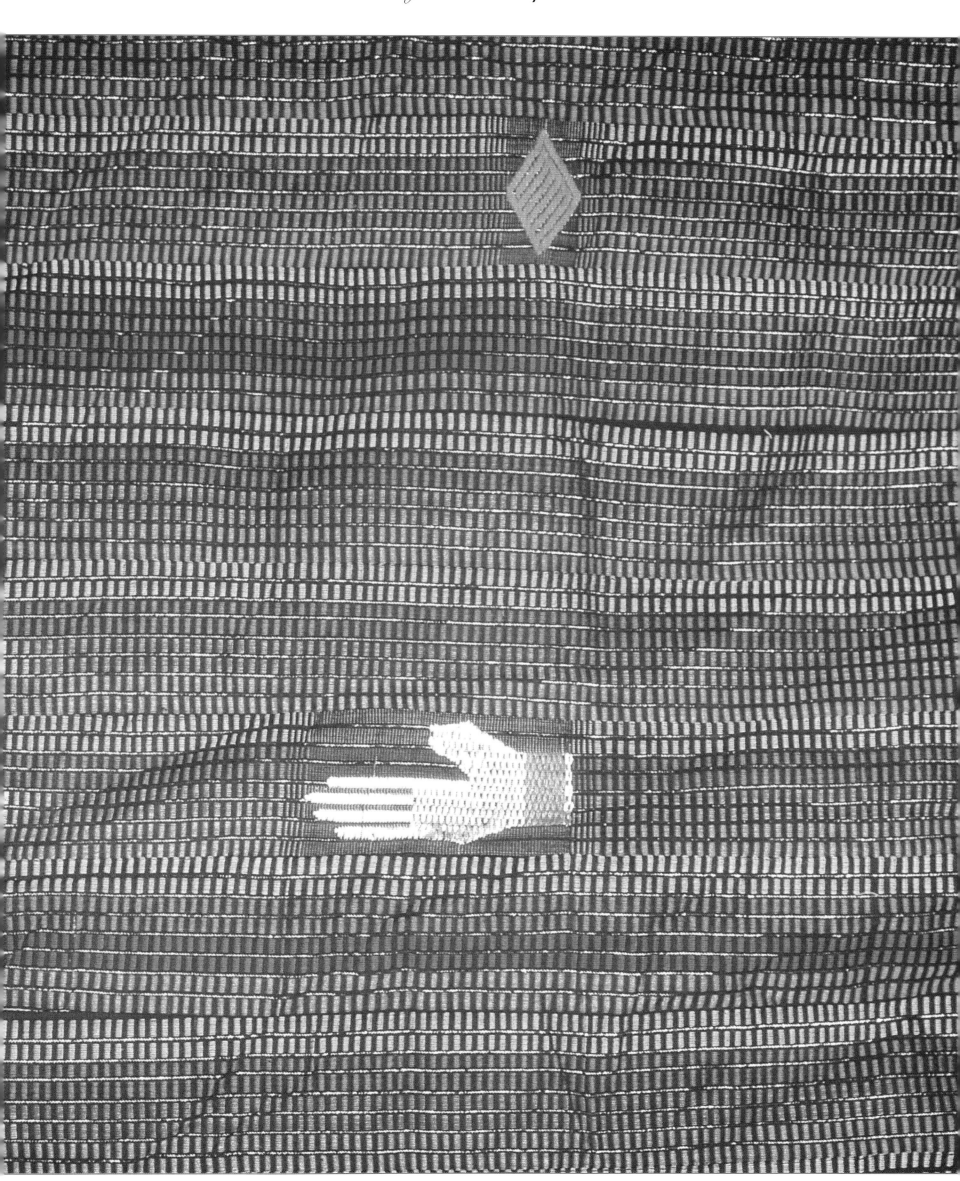

ence on other neighboring peoples, including the Fon of the Benin Republic and most recently the Yoruba of Nigeria. One particularly interesting and distinctive type of Ewe cloth, called *adanudo*, features a rich variety of weft float inlaid pictures, often on a plain silk, rayon, or cotton background. Among the subjects depicted on these cloths are animals such as cows, sheep and horses, human figures, ceremonial stools, hats, trees and flowers, and household objects such as dining forks. More recent examples are often quite realistic, and at least since the 1940s some of the cloths have included written texts. The Ewe weavers also produced many cloths where, as with Ashanti kente, the main design feature is symmetrically arranged blocks of weft float designs and weft-faced stripes across the strips.

While it is relatively easy to tell Ewe cloths made for local sale from those woven by the Ashanti, it becomes far more difficult when Ewe weavers deliberately imitate the style of kente cloth. Many Ewe weavers are entrepreneurial and quite ready to adapt their weaving style and even travel considerable distances in search of a market for their output. It is quite likely that at least some Ewe weavers have been producing their own versions of Ashanti kente for much of the last century, helped by the less discriminating market that developed with the eclipsing of the Kumasi court as primary patron.

ABOVE AND RIGHT (DETAIL)
A men's cotton cloth with alternating sections of warp and weft-faced plain weave and supplementary weft float decoration; twentieth century, Ewe.

However, despite their superficial similarity, these cloths can generally be distinguished from Ashanti weaving by the inclusion of figurative designs of the type described above, and by the use of a technique which involves plying together two colors of weft thread before weaving a band, creating a kind of speckled effect. Another distinctive feature of certain Ewe weaving is the use of a technique called supplementary warp float, where an extra set of warp threads floats along the cloth strip, usually to form stripes of unwoven thread on the surface. This technique, which is extremely rare in African weaving, is not normally used by the Ashanti.

In the last few decades however, as the international demand for kente cloth has grown, many of the Ewe master weavers have established workshops directly to supply the export trade to the United States. Not only do Ewe weavers adopt another style for overseas patrons, they are also prepared to compete with other indigenous weavers for African markets outside Ghana in cities such as Lagos in Nigeria and Dakar in Senegal. Ewe men regard themselves as expert professional weavers who are the best at whatever style they take on. Often this results not in a stale copying but a creative exploration and fusion of older styles with innovations in an effort to meet new markets, contributing to the current vibrancy of African textile design.

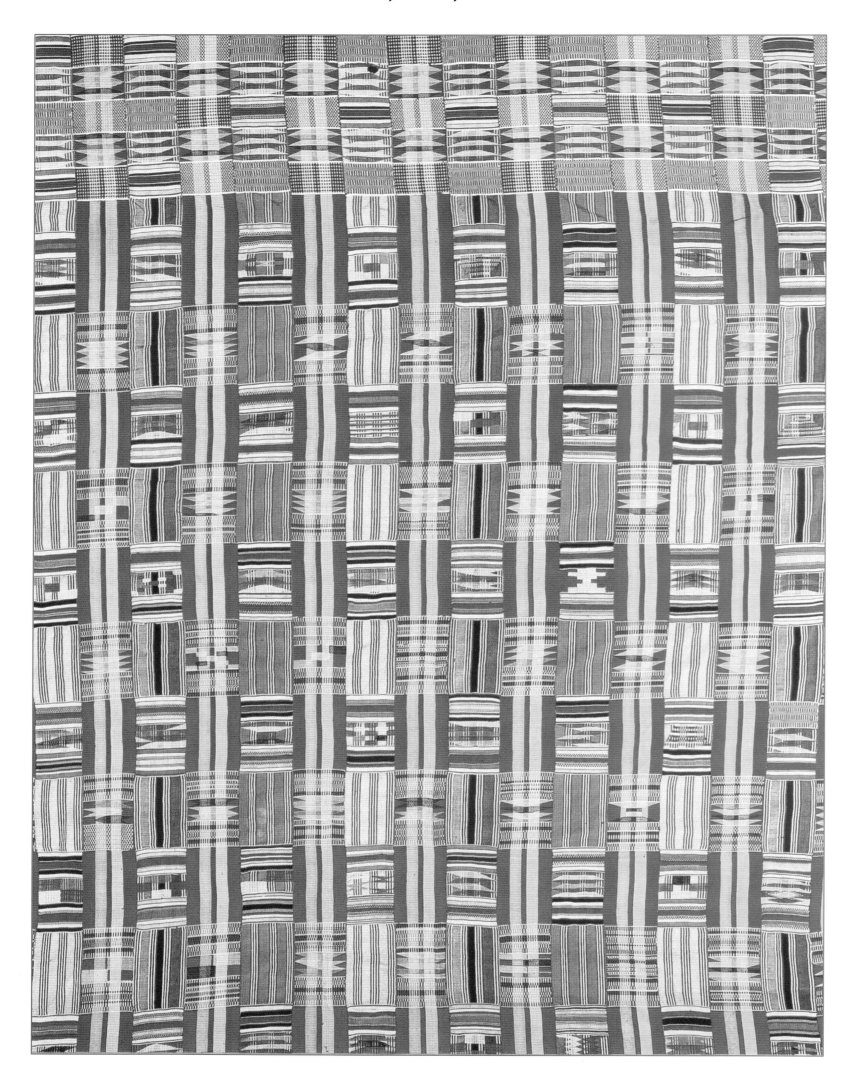

*A men's silk cloth with alternating
sections of warp and weft-faced plain
weave and supplementary weft float
decoration; twentieth century, Ashanti.*

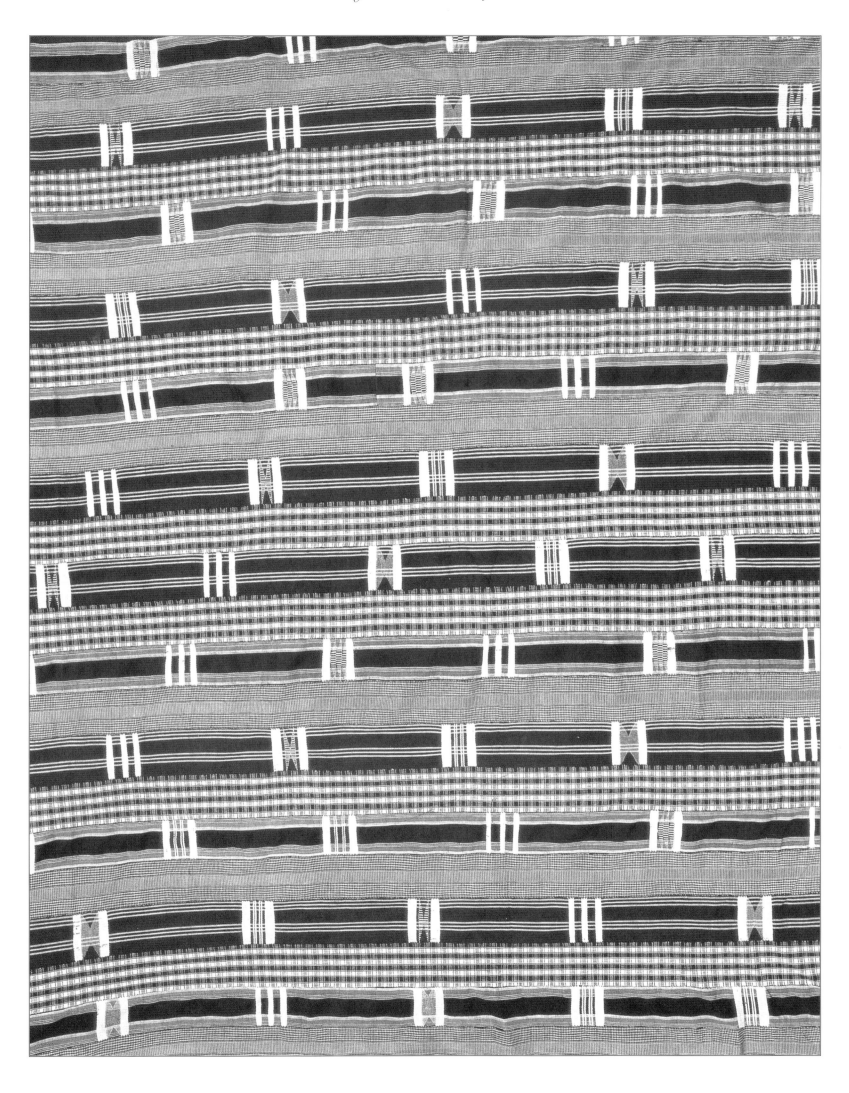

*A men's cotton cloth with supplementary
weft float decoration; twentieth century,
Ashanti.*

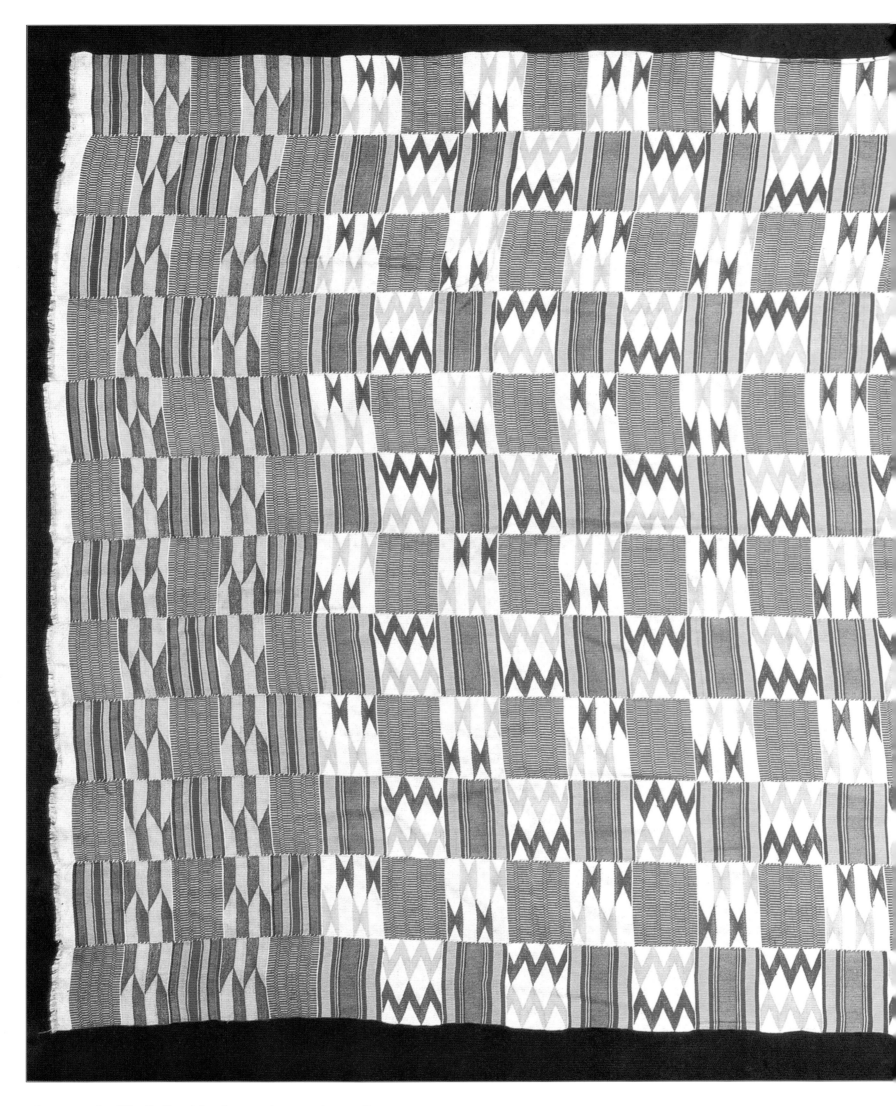

A woman's silk cloth with alternating sections of warp
and weft-faced plain weave and supplementary weft
float decoration; twentieth century, Ashanti.

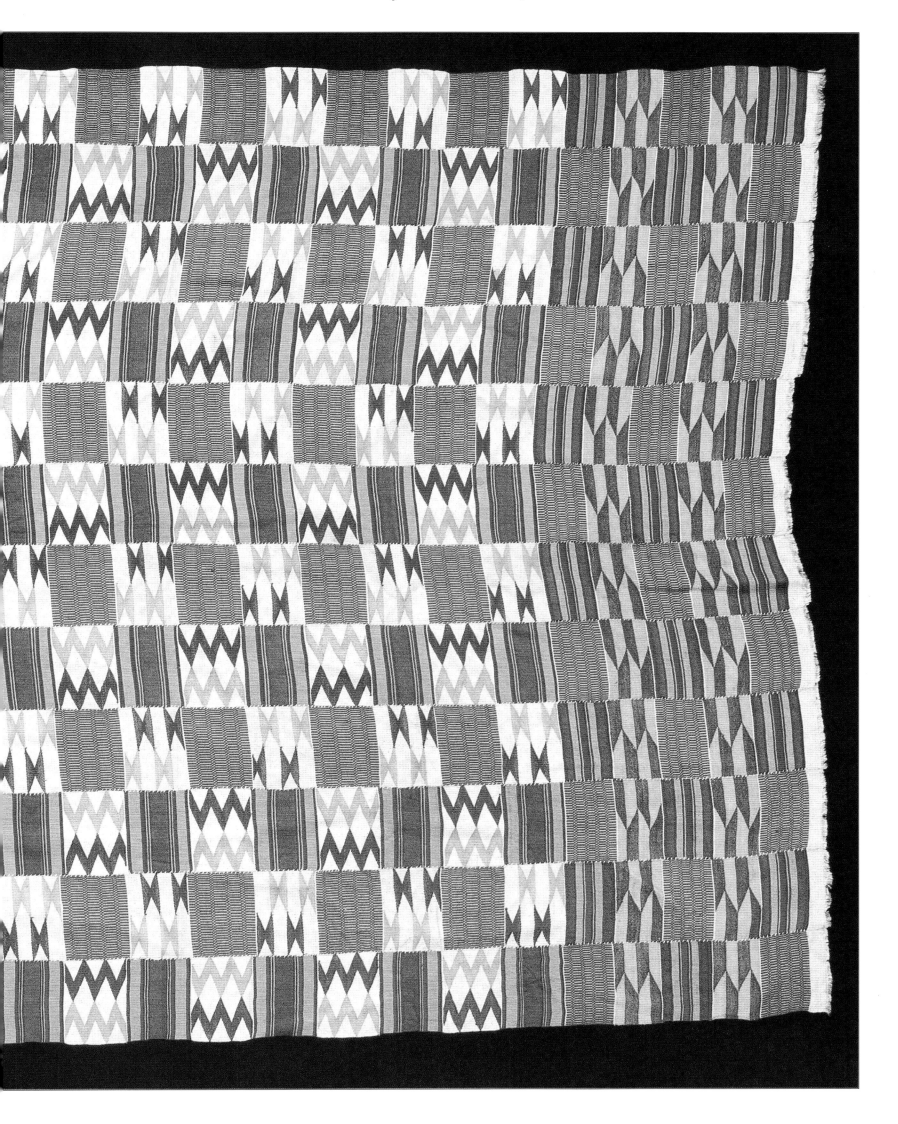

ABOVE
A woman's silk cloth with supplementary weft float decoration; twentieth century, Ashanti.

RIGHT
A men's cotton cloth with alternating sections of warp and weft-faced plain weave and figurative supplementary weft float decoration; twentieth century, Ewe, Volta region of Ghana.

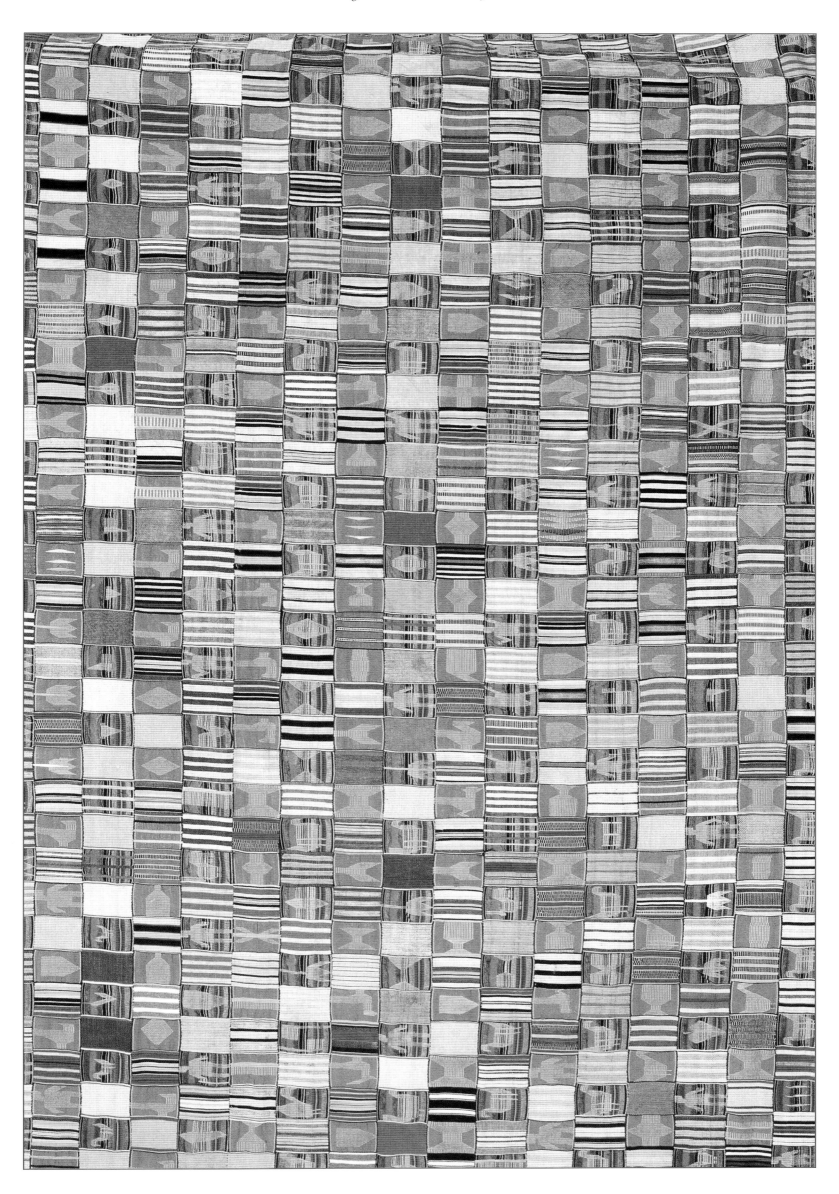

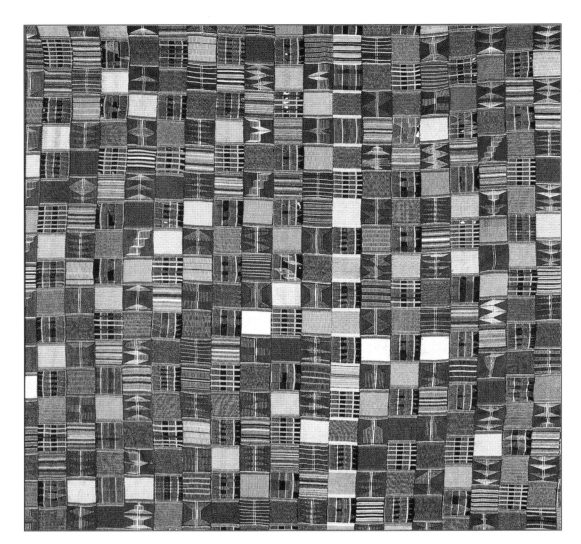

LEFT, BELOW AND RIGHT
Men's cotton cloths with alternating sections of warp and weft-faced plain weave and figurative supplementary weft float decoration; twentieth century, Ewe, Volta region of Ghana.

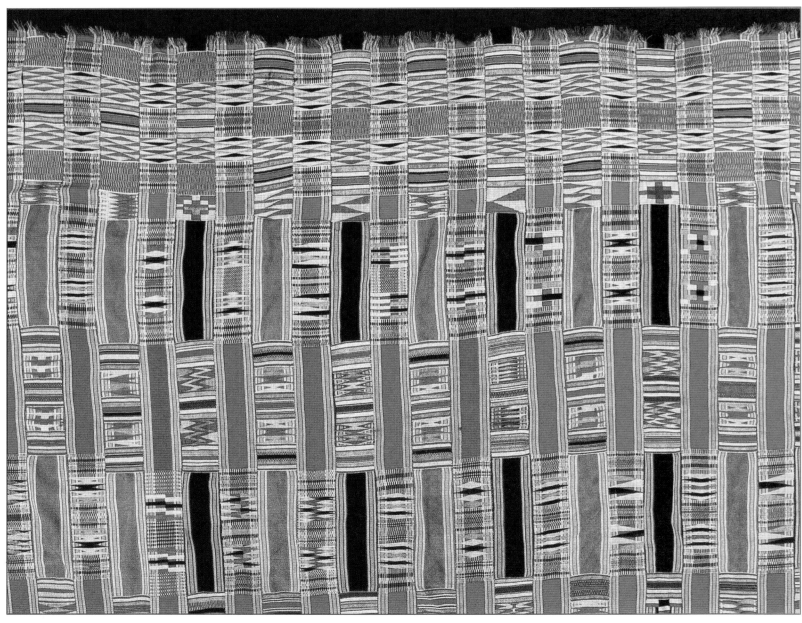

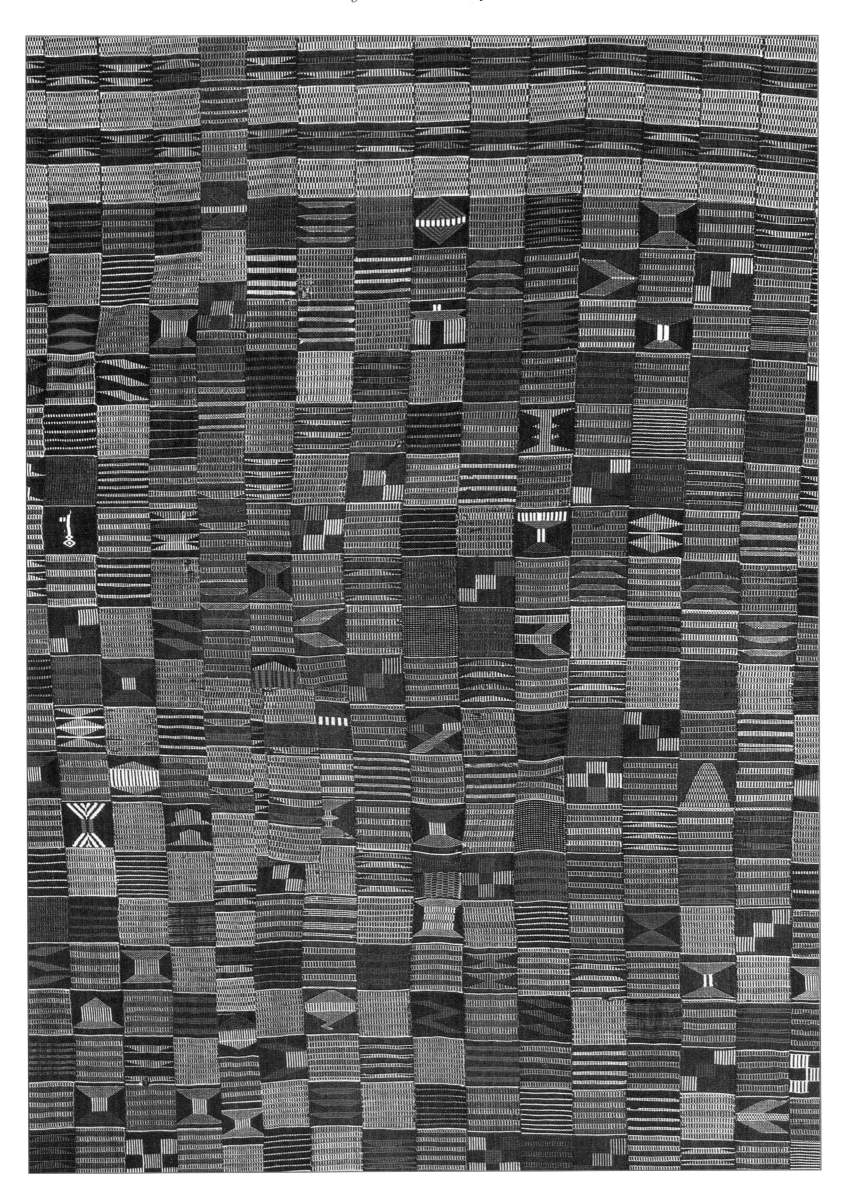

BOGOLAN, MUD-DYED CLOTH OF MALI

If the kente cloth discussed in the previous chapter has long been regarded as the pre-eminent African textile form, its status has recently been challenged from an unexpected quarter. Over the last ten or so years the perception of Bogolan cloth from Mali has been transformed from a despised rural cloth associated with non-Islamic peasants to a symbol of national identity, while internationally its new influence embraces both Parisian interior designers and Afrocentric dress in the United States.

Bogolanfini is a cloth decorated by women in the Bamana-speaking region of Mali, using a unique procedure that utilises dyes made from mud and leaves to produce white designs outlined by a black background. In its local context it remains a crucial garment worn to mark important life-cycle stages including birth, female excision, marriage, and death. In the Malian capital, Bamako, numerous young men have taken up the craft to produce simplified versions of older designs for a growing tourist and international market. Many of these use stencils and chemicals which are far faster than the traditional hand-painting and local dyes. Artists have experimented with the technique as an alternative to painting in oils. Internationally a Paris-based Malian fashion designer achieved widespread recognition when he began to incorporate Bogolan in his

ABOVE (DETAIL) AND RIGHT
Bogolanfini women's wrapper,
mud-dyed hand-woven cloth; Bamana,
Mali, twentieth century.

clothes, starting a vogue for the distinctive designs, which now sees them reproduced from New York to India.

Bogolanfini, which translates from the Bamana as "mud cloth," is a long established tradition among the Bamana, who inhabit a large area to the east and north of Bamako. Islam has been a major force in Mali for many centuries but did not make significant inroads in most Bamana regions until recently and many aspects of ancestral religious and cultural traditions are still thriving, albeit in modified forms. As a consequence they are well known to anthropologists and African art enthusiasts following numerous studies of their artistic and religious heritage, including a rich variety of masquerade forms. It is only in recent years, however, that the techniques of cloth dyeing have been researched and documented. The production of bogolan cloth involves a unique and lengthy procedure, which we can only outline here.

Although bogolan is made throughout the Bamana area, and even by some women from other ethnic groups such as the Dogon and Fulani, the acknowledged experts who produce the best designed and finest cloth come from the Beledougou Bamana area to the north of Bamako. Our description of the technique will be based on research there in the 1970s by

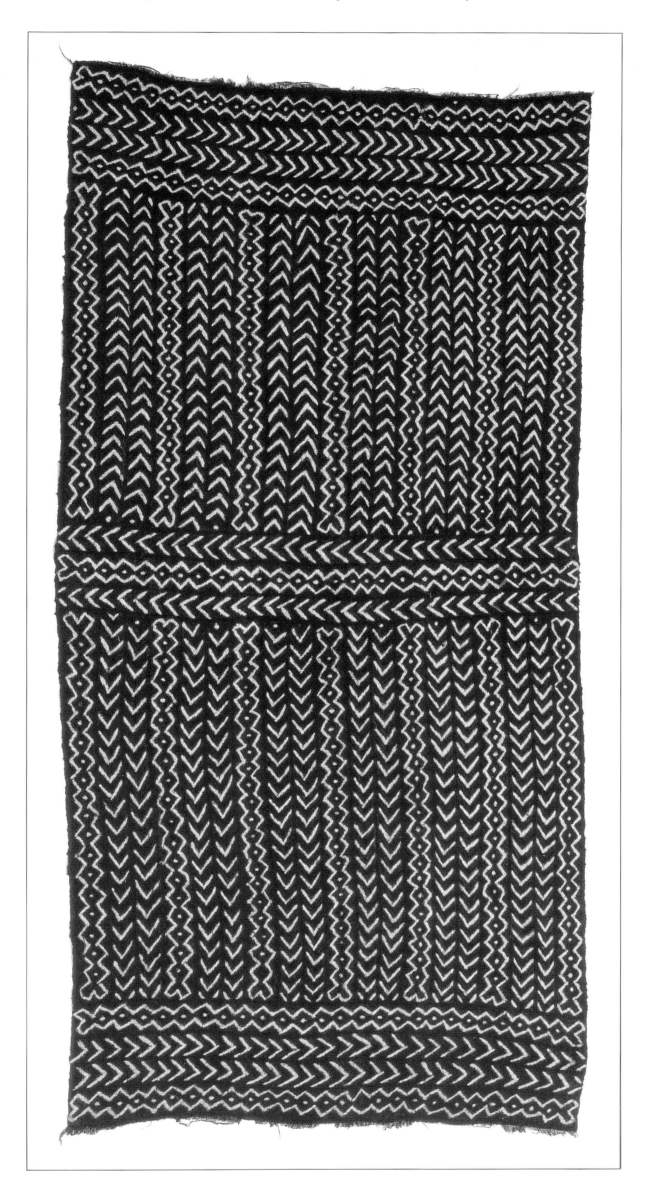

Pascal Imperato and Marli Shamir, and more recent data collected by Tavy Aherne. The raw material is provided by plain white cotton cloth woven by men on the local version of the narrow strip loom found throughout most of West Africa. The undyed cloth strips, about twelve centimetres wide, are still sewn up into shirts and robes and used as everyday dress by men in the country areas, although factory-produced cloth is increasingly widely used instead. The plain cloth that is to be turned into bogolan is first sewn up into a woman's wrapper cloth or whatever other garment the customer requires. There are apparently four recognized colors of bogolan produced in Beledougou: black, gray, red, and white, but we will concentrate here on the black which is by far the most common.

Although men in Bamako have taken up bogolan dyeing in recent years, in the Beledougou area it remains primarily a women's craft passed on from mother to daughter. The cloth is first washed in water and allowed to dry so that it can shrink to its final size. It is then soaked in a brown solution made from the pounded leaves of certain trees. Although the main leaves used are widely known, specialists have their own closely guarded recipes to give the best results. Once the cloth has been soaked in the mixture it takes on a deep even yellow color which fades only slightly when it is spread out on the ground to dry in the sun. It is now ready for the mud dye to be applied. The mud used is collected from the very deepest sections of the ponds which become exposed for a few months at the height of the dry season. This mud is left to ferment in a covered pot for about a year, during which time it becomes black. When it is needed, some mud is taken from the pot and diluted with water.

Small pieces of bamboo and flat metal spatula of various widths are used to draw the design onto the cloth using the mud solution. There are several stages to the design process. First the woman marks off the main sections of the design she has in mind, dividing up the cloth into areas to be filled in with patterns. This is done with the cloth spread flat on the ground, but for the next stages of more detailed work, she sits and draws the part of the cloth to be painted over a large calabash in her lap. Next she outlines the designs in the section, using a very thin spatula to draw the edges of the required patterns. When all the designs in that section have been drawn in outline, she then uses a wider implement to fill in the mud dye over the spaces left between them. One of the unique features of high quality bogolan is that it is the background, not the designs themselves, that are painted onto the cloth, leaving the design in the remaining undyed areas. It can take several weeks of slow and painstaking work before the whole cloth is covered. The cloth is then washed with water to remove any excess mud leaving a black background from which the yellow designs stand out. The whole process of dipping the cloth in the leaf solution and outlining the designs with a layer of black mud dye is then repeated, giving the cloth a second coating of dye. The final stage is to apply a solution that includes caustic soda to the yellow areas so that they are bleached to the desired white. The solution is carefully painted onto the undyed sections of the cloth, turning them first to a shade of brown. It is only when the cloth is left out in the fierce sunlight for a week that they become white and the cloth is completed. There are various aspects that allow a well executed bogolanfini to be distinguished from a more hurried job or the work of a less skilled artist. These include the balance of the overall composition, the deepness and fastness of the black color, the sureness of the lines, and the absence of tool marks and unevenness in the dyed areas. Local experts are apparently able to distinguish the individual style of certain artists and these women may become well known and attract clients from a considerable distance. By contrast much of the bogolan now made in Bamako for the tourist trade and the export market is hastily produced using stencils and simplified designs, often with the addition of chemicals to the dyeing process.

It would seem strange to begin with a white cloth, dye it to yellow, then finish up by treating the yellow areas so they become white again. The reason for this apparently paradoxical procedure lies in the chemical processes at work in the dyeing process. The active ingredient in the mud dye is iron oxide, which is converted by tannic acid in the leaf solution into a fast dye of iron

ABOVE AND BELOW
Bogolanfini women's wrapper, mud-dyed hand-woven cloth; Bamana, Mali, twentieth century.

tannate. The yellow stage is therefore essential although as a color it is not present on the finished cloth.

Within the local tradition of bogolan cloth-making in the countryside it does not appear that artists were usually expected to produce innovatory designs. Rather the mark of a successful design was the reproduction of existing designs clearly, and perhaps in some novel but appropriate combination. Many of the individual motifs applied to sections of the cloth, or combinations of these motifs, have names, which are apparently quite widely known. Some of these names are based on the appearance of the pattern, such as "fish bones," "little stars," or "square." A few refer to historical events — according to recent research by Tavy Aherne one complex design that is named after the "fighting ground between the iguana and the squirrel at the Woyowayanko river" recalls a battle fought between the French colonialists and the Bamana leader Samory. A common pattern of a cross shape set diagonally within a square is called "Mauretanian woman's head-cushion" after the expensive embroidered leather cushions such women own and has implications of both femininity and wealth. A few designs have names which refer to aspects of women's daily experience, in particular to issues such as co-wives, rivalry within polygamous households.

It is important however not to overstress the role of these names, which may in many cases be subject to local or regional variations. Although the designs may be recognised as named patterns, recalling the individual, object, or event in question, in the majority of cases they do not seem to be symbolic in a deeper sense bound up with the use of the cloth. Nor can the overall designs of most cloths be "read" to form a coherent text. Nevertheless it has been suggested that in some of the most important contexts of local use, notably in the cloths designed to be worn by young women in the period of confinement following excision ceremonies, the design of the cloth can be understood as related to their use. Two specific designs of cloth were worn by these women to protect them from hostile spiritual forces during the potentially dangerous stages of transition into adulthood before being entrusted to the care of the elderly woman who had looked after the initiates. Different but related ideas about protection from danger and the absorption of potentially harmful powers underlie the other main context in which bogolan was still worn in a traditional context, namely by hunters when confronting and killing powerful animals.

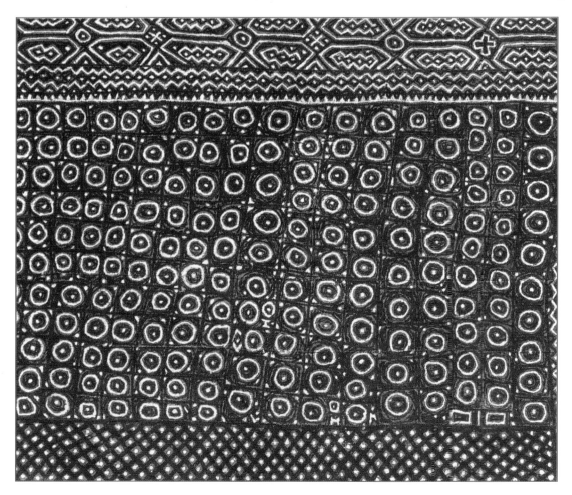

RIGHT
Wax-resist cloth with a design inspired by bogolanfini, manufactured by Sotiba, Senegal, in the 1990s.

LEFT
Bogolanfini women's wrapper, mud-dyed hand-woven cloth; Bamana, Mali, twentieth century.

Although the recent promotion of bogolan from this rural context was far removed from the concerns of the Bamana, it none the less draws on ideas of cultural heritage and tradition based on a sense that the cloth brings with it a part of these associations of a rural African authenticity. The new role for bogolan has its roots with two separate streams of developments in Bamako involving local fine artists and fashion designers. At the art schools in Bamako young artists began to experiment with and research the technique as part of an ideological commitment to the use of local materials in their work. These moves led in the 1980s to the formation of a collective of six artists calling themselves Groupe Bogolan Kasobane, who went on to exhibit widely — in Europe and Francophone Africa — an increasing variety of both abstract and representational works that utilised the bogolan technique. The pioneer of the use of bogolan in fashion design was Malian designer Chris Seydou working in Paris. After attracting much interest with a wrap of bogolan in his 1979 show, he rapidly increased the use of the fabric through the 1980s and early 1990s. When wealthy Bamako customers saw the new styles he was creating using the fabric, and realised how much interest it was attracting abroad, the response was enthusiastic. Seydou, before his early death in 1994, promoted bogolan through annual fashion shows on Malian television and worked with local textile factories to develop industrially manufactured versions of the mud cloth designs. Tourists attracted to Mali in increasing numbers by interest in other aspects of the country's artistic heritage, from the ancient terracottas of old Jenne to the success of musicians like Salif Keita, added to the demand. Students and other young people in Bamako wore bogolan in home-made copies of Seydou's expensive dresses. Local musicians adopted bogolan for their stage costumes. Unemployed graduates began to mass-produce simplified versions to supply the growing export trade. Today bogolan hats, waistcoats, and jackets can be bought in the markets of New York and London while higher priced styles dominate the work of fashion designers following in Seydou's footsteps in the capitals of Francophone Africa from Dakar to Niamey.

Bogolan can be seen in even less likely places too. In India textile factories are turning out cheap bedspreads based on bogolan designs, while in France an exclusive company makes expensive towels, sheets, and bathrobes with the now familiar black and white designs. Although the tendency is for foreign observers to be disturbed by the supposed commercialisation of African traditions, ignoring the benefits to the country and people concerned in terms of much needed employment and a higher international profile, the work of artists and designers using bogolan has demonstrated that in this case at least success need not mean an end to artistic creativity.

RIGHT AND BELOW
Bogolan with simplified designs and modified technique produced in the 1990s by young men in Bamako for the tourist market.

ASO OKE, CEREMONIAL CLOTH OF THE YORUBA

The Yoruba now form one of the most numerous ethnic groups in Africa, inhabiting the southwestern part of Nigeria, with smaller numbers across the border in the Benin Republic and Togo. Significant numbers of people of Yoruba origin may also be found throughout the Americas and in parts of Europe following the slave trade and more recent diasporas. Although the Yoruba were never united under a single political authority, the common elements of their linguistic and cultural heritage have provided a legacy which in the twentieth century has provided the basis for a growing sense of ethnic unity. Two key elements of this heritage are the political charter for Yoruba kingship provided by the myth of descent from the king of an ancestral city, Ife, and a richly complex set of religious practices.

Yoruba mythology holds that the founding kings of all the ancient Yoruba kingdoms were the sons of Oduduwa, who climbed down from heaven to found the world at Ife. Ife itself seems to have flourished as a wealthy city-state from about the twelfth to the fifteenth century A.D., retaining some kind of spiritual authority long after its temporal power had declined. The

ABOVE (DETAIL) AND RIGHT
*A compound of Yoruba aso oke weavers
in the town of Iseyin, 1994.*

wealth and culture of ancient Ife is demonstrated by the extraordinary brass and terracotta sculptures left behind by its royal court. When these were discovered by Europeans early in the twentieth century the great German ethnographer Leo Frobenius was convinced that he had found the fabled lost city of Atlantis. Ife is also the centre of the cult of Ifa, the complex and sophisticated divination system that is at the intellectual core of Yoruba religious traditions. Yoruba religion has been a major contributor to religions of African origin in the Americas, most notably to Haitian voodoo, Cuban Santeria, and Brazilian Candomble, largely due to the predominance of Yoruba captives in the final decades of the trans-Atlantic slave trade in the nineteenth century. However, from about the sixteenth century the temporal power of Ife was surpassed by the Yoruba cavalry power of the kingdom of Oyo to the northwest and the growing empire of the Edo people of Benin to the southeast, although the rulers of both of these states claimed descent from the founders of Ife.

The king of Oyo, the Alafin, along with the rulers of lesser states, maintained an elaborate palace and court ceremonial that was the major

patron for Yoruba artists working in a huge range of media including wood sculptors, leather workers, calabash carvers, drummers, court historians, iron workers, and brass casters, as well as weavers, tailors, and embroiderers. The cults of the various deities, known as *orisha*, and of masquerades such as Egungun and Gelede, were also active patrons of the arts. Cloth was central to the social, religious, political, economic, and cultural life of these complex and sophisticated communities. The significance of cloth is stressed by an account of the origin of clothing in the texts memorized by the diviners of the the Ifa system. It tells how there was dissension and strife in the family that went about naked. Finally the father consulted Ifa and was told to make sacrifices to Eshu, the messenger of the gods. Eshu then taught the man to harvest cotton and have it woven into clothing. Once his family saw him dressed they were respectful of his orders and social harmony was restored. Cloth became one of the main indicators of social status and wealth, ranked with children and good health as the markers of a life fulfilled.

The Yoruba-speaking region of Nigeria is one where two forms of weaving technology overlap and both the upright single-heddle loom and the narrow-strip double-heddle loom are found. The evidence, including the discovery of fragments of cloth in archaeological contexts at Benin and Igbo Ukwu (circa ninth century A.D.), suggests that the upright loom is of great antiquity in the area, while the narrow strip loom is one of several aspects of Yoruba culture probably introduced into Oyo via contacts with northern trade routes. Weaving on the upright loom was the work of women who mobilised their daughters and junior sisters as spinners and trainees to produce large quantities of indigo and white-striped cloths for everyday use. The basic indigo and white cloths, known as *kijipa*, were also widely traded in huge quantities both via overland trade routes to the north, and to European merchants on the coast.

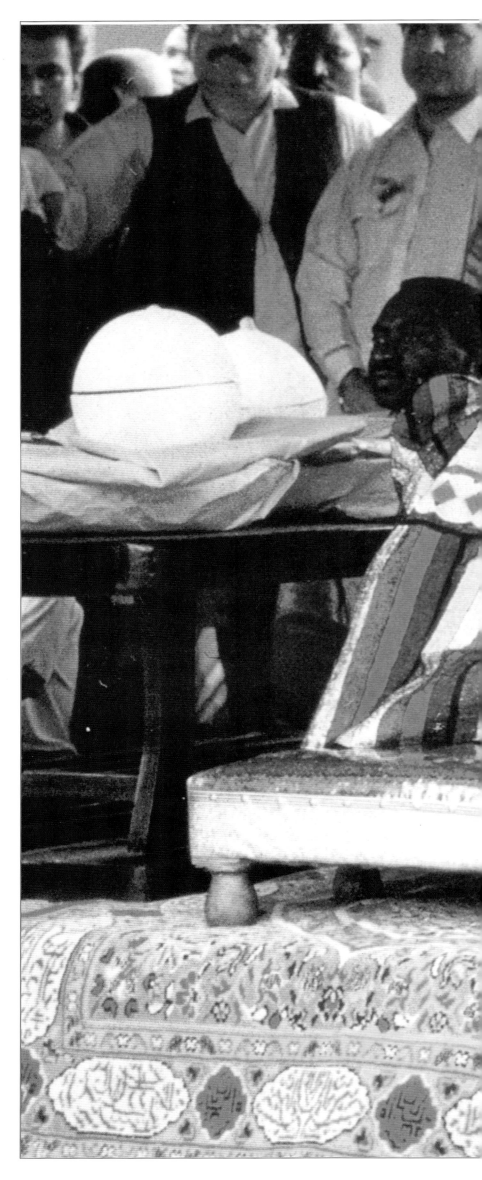

RIGHT
One of the most senior kings, His Majesty Oba Lamidi Olayiwola Adeyemi III, the Alafin of Oyo, wearing a new aso oke robe as he prepares to confer a chieftaincy title; Oyo, Nigeria, July 1995.

From the seventeenth century European traders brought Yoruba cloths from Ijebu and Benin middlemen and shipped them for resale in the Gold Coast, Congo, and even to clothe the slave population of Brazil. As well as the kijipa, weavers on this type of loom in the various parts of the Yoruba region created numerous more localized styles of more highly decorated cloths for a variety of ritual and ceremonial uses. These included different types of marriage cloths and red cloths for chiefly funerals among the north-eastern Bunu, a wide range of cloths for weddings and ceremonies for elders in Owo, and the aso olona of the Ijebu Yoruba discussed earlier. There is some evidence that some of the more ritually important of these cloths may have been woven by men, despite the more general prohibition on men using this type of loom. In the twentieth century a variety of factors including declining demand, the new access to education for young women, and alternative employment opportunities, have contributed to a dramatic decline in upright loom weaving among the Yoruba. A few weavers still make some of the ceremonial cloths, particularly in Ijebu-ode, but elsewhere the tradition has become virtually defunct.

In marked contrast to the fate of upright loom weaving, Yoruba aso oke weaving on the narrow-strip loom is without doubt one of the most vibrant and successful artistic traditions in Africa today. It was not until the 1820s that Europeans reached the interior of Yorubaland, so earlier direct evidence for this type of weaving is reliant on reports from slave traders on the coast. In a book published in 1823, one Captain Adams, who made several voyages to the region between 1786 and 1800, wrote that "the cloth manufactured in Hio [i.e. Oyo] is superior, both for variety of pattern, color, and dimensions, to any made in the neighbouring states." At the height of its power in the eighteenth century Oyo maintained a substantial trade in textiles with neighboring peoples, as well as supplying the needs of the wealthiest of the Yoruba kings. The nineteenth century, however, saw the fall of Oyo in the face of internal conflicts and the attacks of Fulani-led Islamic jihadists from the north. Oyo itself was abandoned in the 1830s, with a successor king later re-establishing the city to the south. The dispersal of weavers in the course of this movement and the decades of war that followed led to the spread of narrow-strip weaving throughout the Yoruba and the establishment of

LEFT
Alhaji Kegunhe, a wealthy master weaver in Iseyin, displays part of his store of cloth; 1996.

RIGHT
Alhaji Moshood, a leading Oyo master weaver, with his daughter on the occasion of the naming ceremony for her child. Their aso oke outfits combine the traditional beige colour once popular in wild silk, with the latest in lurex designs; Oyo, 1996.

large communities of weavers in the towns of Iseyin and Ilorin.

Today the tradition of aso oke weaving inherited from the upheavals of the nineteenth century centers around three prestige cloths: *etu*, *sanyan*, and *alaari* — although in reality a far wider range of designs were woven in the past. These three cloths are still associated with a deep sense of respect for tradition and a consciousness of identity as Yorubas, although they have long since been supplanted by more recent fashions. Etu is a deep blue, almost black, indigo-dyed cloth, so dark that a costly dyeing process involving many, many immersions in the pot of indigo was needed. The dark blue is offset by very thin warp and weft stripes, often only a single thread in width, of lighter blue. The name etu means guinea fowl, and the cloth is likened to the bird's speckled plumage. A verse from a Ifa divination text describes etu as the father of all cloths, while proverbs note the respect it inspires in viewers, asserting for example that a man whose head has worn an etu cap should never again carry a load. Sanyan is woven from the beige silk obtained throughout Nigeria from the cocoons of the Anaphe moth, forming a rather uneven pale brown cloth, often with a narrow white stripe down the centre of each strip. Alaari is the Yoruba name for cloth woven using the magenta waste silk imported across the Sahara from Tripoli. Cloths woven entirely with this silk were extremely rare and it was more usual to weave it as stripes of weft float decorations into an indigo-dyed cloth.

In the nineteenth and early part of the twentieth century these three cloths were an important part of an inter-regional trade network that extended northward far beyond the Yoruba to encompass Nupe weavers and embroiderers, Hausa embroiderers and tailors, and aristocratic Fulani patrons in the supply of prestige robes and trousers to kings, emirs, and chiefs throughout a huge expanse of West Africa. The Islamic-influenced dress styles, elaborated by the Yoruba into a huge range of types of robes and trousers, gradually supplanted the earlier form of men's dress based on tied and wrapped cloths. Women, however, retained the older style, modifying it with additional cloths and the introduction of a sewn blouse in the twentieth century.

ABOVE (DETAIL) AND LEFT
Aso oke women's cloth, machine-spun cotton with silk weft floats in the 1930s/40s at Ilorin, Nigeria.

Although sanyan, etu, and alaari remain at the centre of the aso oke tradition, in the last century the shift in power from the "traditional rulers" to new elites has been mirrored by a shift in the centres of patronage for aso oke weavers. Today, although the cloth is bought for certain occasions by all Yoruba, the most important customers and leaders of fashion are the wealthy educated elites of cities such as Lagos and Ibadan. In the early decades of this century they set the pattern for wearing aso oke which, with certain fluctuations, persists today and sustains an expanding community of weavers. At the turn of the century African society in Lagos was dominated by a select group of families most of whom were Saro, that is descendants of Yoruba who had been taken to Freetown in Sierra Leone after being rescued by the British navy from slave ships off the coast. Many of these people, who converted to Christianity and received an English education from missionaries in Freetown, chose to return to Lagos after it became a colony in the 1860s. As a wealthy minority able to interact more closely with the new English colonial regime they were widely imitated and the fashion for European dress spread rapidly, assisted by missionary activities and a growing colonial presence throughout Yorubaland. However, although most Saro dressed and behaved as black Englishmen and women, holding garden parties and tea dances, by the 1890s there was a vocal minority calling for a return to African names and styles of dress. This sense of cultural nationalism had a gradual impact on fashionable dress for ceremonial occasions. Particularly important for the future of aso oke weaving was a custom called *aso ebi*, which probably originated in Freetown, but became popular in Yoruba cities by the 1920s. This involves groups of celebrants at any event expressing their sense of group or family unity by dressing in the same pattern of fabric. Depending on the tastes and wealth of those involved, and the fashion of the day, this fabric could be imported wax prints, velvet, or lace, but most often it was aso oke.

By the middle of the twentieth century the pattern for wearing aso oke as a special cloth for important and ceremonial occasions had been set. By this time locally woven cloth had been almost entirely displaced from everyday wear by imported factory-produced textiles (two excep-

LEFT
Aso oke women's cloth, machine-spun cotton with silk weft floats; Ilorin, Nigeria, 1930s/40s.

RIGHT
Aso oke cloth, hand-spun and machine-spun cotton, from the 1940s/50s. Cloths with this pattern of stripes were given to a bride by the groom's family in the town of Ilorin. Three matching cloths, for the wrapper, shawl, and headtie, made up a complete outfit, together with a blouse of imported cloth.

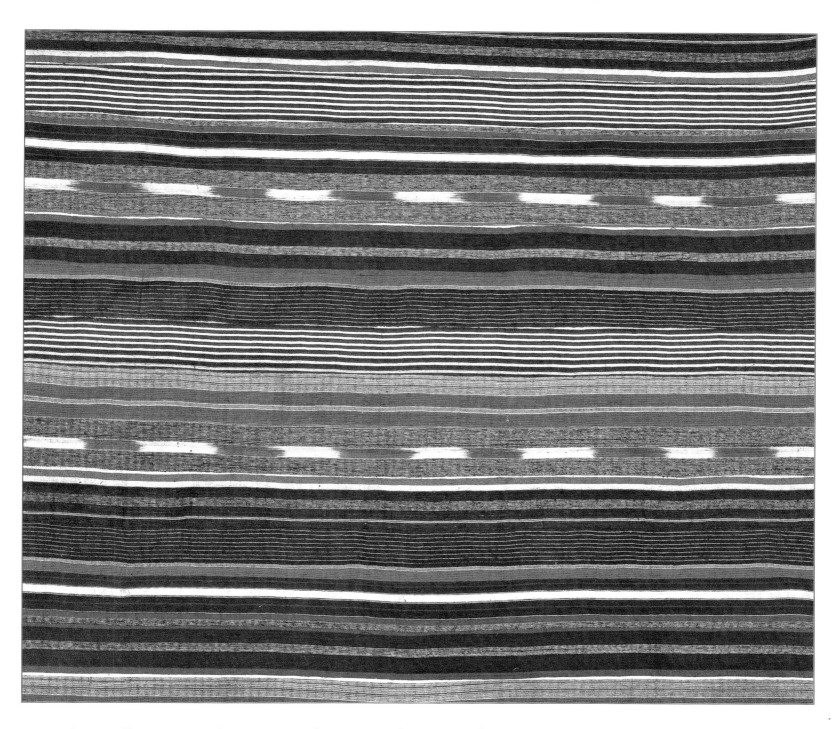

tions that still persist today are men's caps and the cloths which mothers use to support babies on their backs.) Aso oke was worn at life-cycle events such as naming ceremonies for babies, engagements, weddings, important birthdays, chieftaincy title ceremonies, and funerals, as well as the major festivals and Christian or Islamic holy days. Social clubs were also important patrons of aso oke for their annual dances and other events. One of the reasons aso oke has not received as much recognition abroad as other African styles such as kente is the sheer variety of colors and styles embraced by rapidly changing fashions, utilising an ever wider range of imported and locally produced machine-spun cotton thread and rayon imitation silk. Never the less there are a quite limited set of techniques that underlie the huge and increasing diversity of patterns. *Ikat*, the resist-dyeing of sections of the

warp thread, was popular until the 1960s when machine-spun thread in a range of colours displaced local dyeing. Supplementary weft float or brocade patterning is common, with designs of triangles, combs, Koranic boards, checks, and more rarely writing or figurative designs floating on the top face of the cloth. The most distinctive feature of much aso oke is a form of openwork in which holes are created by using extra weft threads to tie together groups of warps, with the extra wefts themselves forming a pattern on the cloth surface. The basic designs in a majority of cloths however are formed by patterns of warp and, more rarely, weft stripes, and it was these which provided the basis for an elaborate repertoire of pattern names.

Since the mid-1970s the appearance of aso oke has been transformed by the increasing use of Japanese lurex, a metalized plastic fibre

103

which can be woven into the cloth in a variety of ways to create a glittery light-catching effect. This has proved extremely popular with Yoruba customers and is particularly effective under artificial lights at the huge all-night parties that accompany many Yoruba celebrations. The adaptability weavers have displayed in matching the changing tastes of a sophisticated and fash-ion-conscious patronage has been demonstrated again in the 1990s when weavers have responded to competition from Ghanaian Ewe weavers mov-ing into Lagos with further innovations, includ-ing a shift towards weaving wider strips and the introduction of a technique of warp float decora-tion. Such has been the demand for aso oke that the tens of thousands of full time male weavers in Yoruba cities are being joined by increasing numbers of young women. In many ways this cloth, which draws on and contributes to a devel-oping sense of tradition but shifts in style with dazzling rapidity, is more representative of the complexity and diversity of modern Africa than some of the more staid forms we have considered in previous chapters.

ABOVE AND RIGHT (DETAIL)
Trousers made from hand and machine spun silk and cotton indigo-dyed etu cloth, one of the three most prestigious aso oke designs, embroidered with imported silk. This type of wide baggy trousers, worn under a big flowing robe, was introduced into northern Nigeria by Muslim traders from the Sahel, becoming the costume of rulers throughout the Sokoto Caliphate and its neighbors from the eighteenth century. Today they are still worn by chiefs and kings on ceremonial occasions. These were made this century.

TOP
Cotton bridal cloth with writing in supplementary weft float. The text translates as "May God spread the happiness of the bride, Amen." This style of cloth was popular in the late 1940s and 1950s.

LEFT
Women's cotton cloth, with alternate strips of rayon supplementary weft float designs and openwork. Openwork is one of the distinctive features of Yoruba aso oke weaving and is rarely found on narrow-strip cloth elsewhere in Africa; c. 1960s.

RIGHT
Detail of weft-float decoration on a women's ipele or wrapper cloth. Cotton and rayon, Ilorin; c. 1960s.

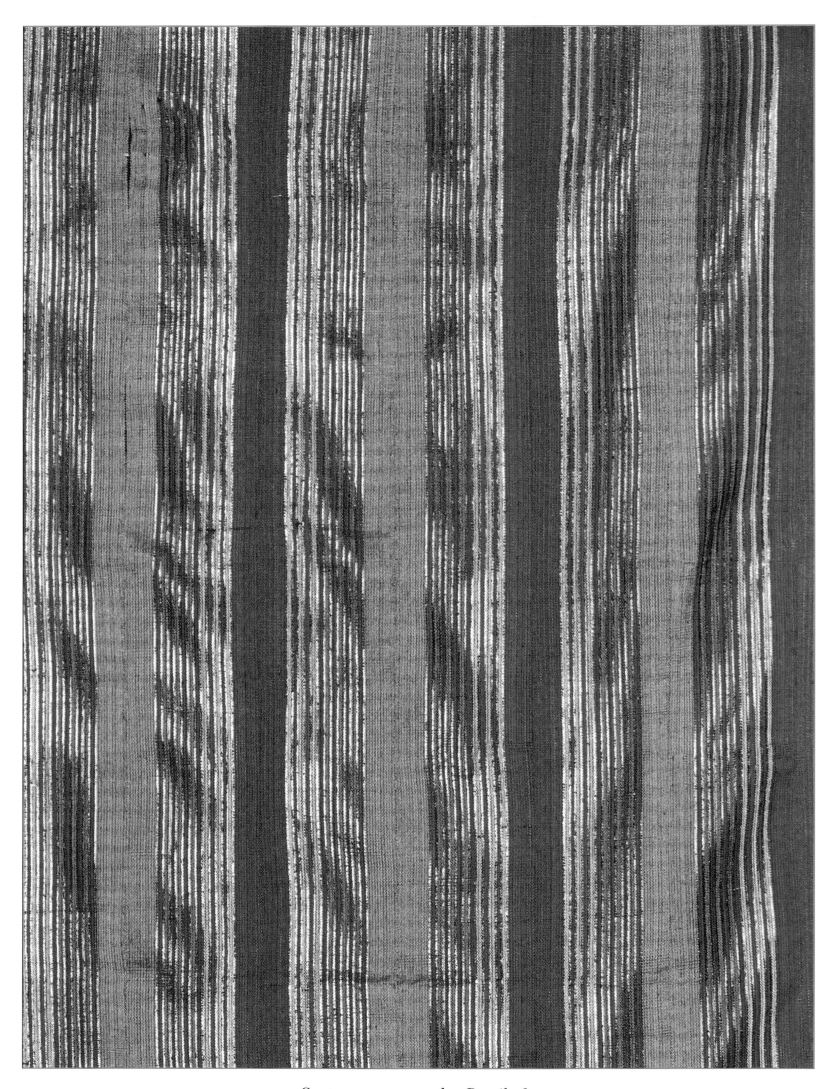

*Contemporary aso oke. Detail of a
woman's head-tie cloth woven in 1994
from cotton, rayon, and lurex.*

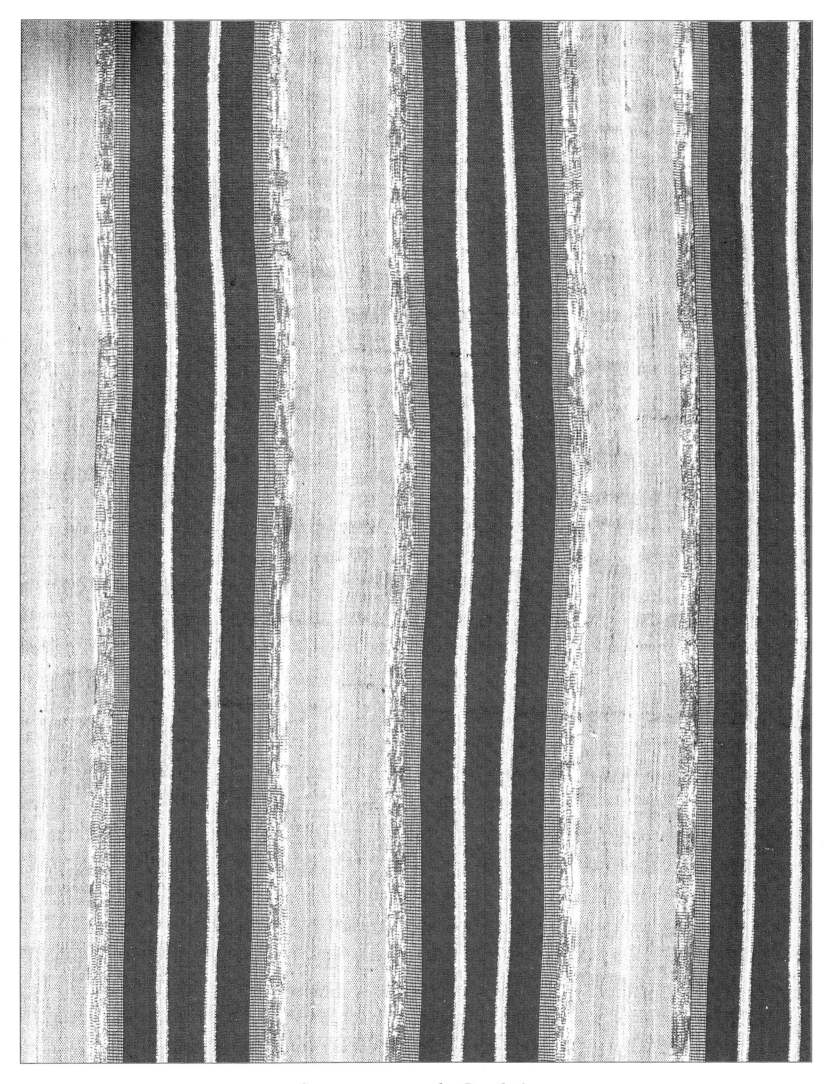

*Contemporary aso oke. Detail of a
women's wrapper cloth woven in Oyo
from cotton and lurex, 1996.*

*Women's wrapper in cotton, rayon, and lurex with
supplementary warp-float decoration. Woven by Ewe
weavers in the Lagos suburb of Ikotun, 1996. They
migrated from Ghana to the Lagos area to compete in
the aso oke market.*

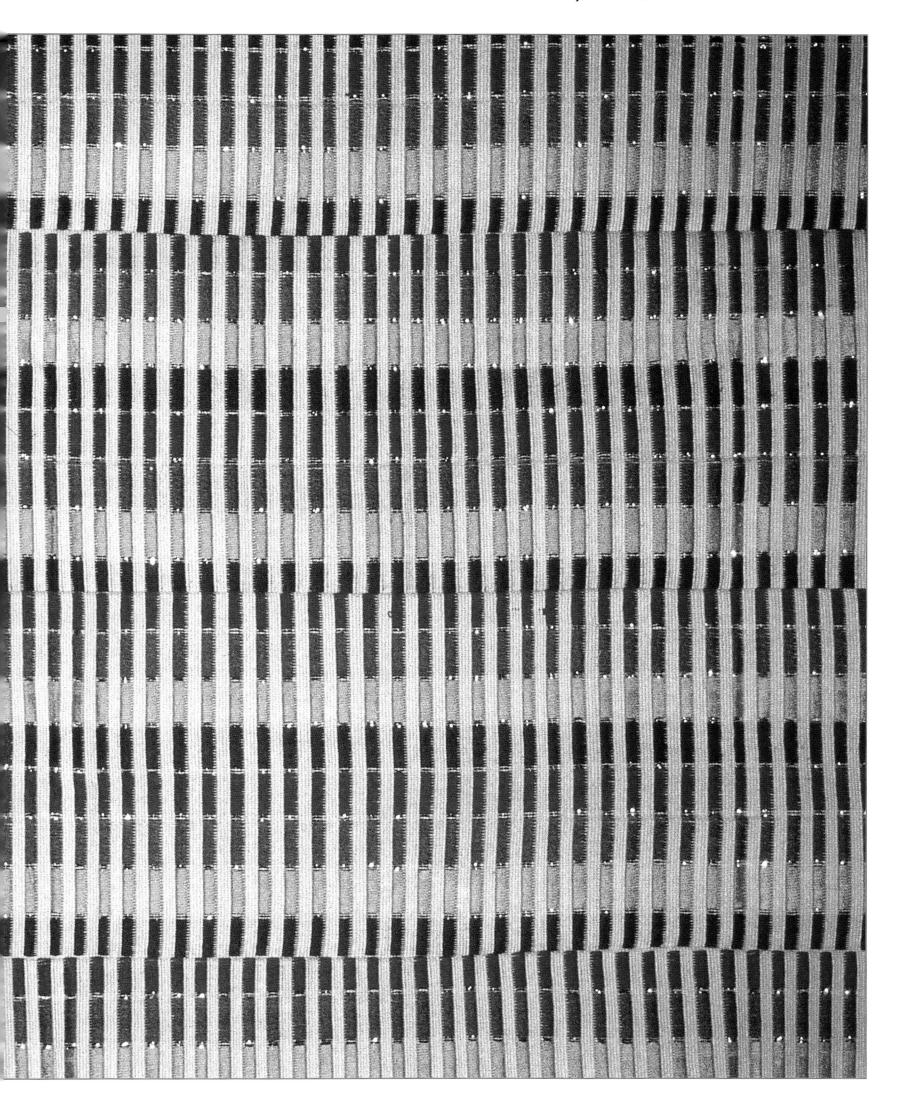

AFRICAN WAX-PRINTED CLOTHS

If the hand-woven and decorated textiles we have described so far in this book represent the heritage of the African past, the vibrant colors and flamboyant designs of wax-printed cloth are more evocative of the Africa of today. Wax-printed cloth and cheaper roller-printed imitations have become one of the most widely distributed forms of African textiles today, produced and worn in almost every country in sub-Saharan Africa. In the process they have become intricately entwined with local social and political life despite their external origin and factory production. Their complex history, linking together Europe, Africa, and southern Asia, has only recently begun to be seriously investigated. Many of the interesting questions they raise about local variations in tastes and color preferences have yet to be answered. Aside from its aesthetic interest, however, we do know that they have provided a new and versatile means of elaborating long-standing African interests in the communicative and expressive power of dress. Governments and political parties have used it to

ABOVE (DETAIL) AND RIGHT
Wax print cotton textile. An early sample of the design known as "Staff of kingship" or "Corkscrew," based on an Ashanti royal sword captured by the British in the Anglo-Ashanti wars. Known to have been in production since 1904. Printed by the Haarlem Cotton Company.

promote their leaders and policies, while at the other extreme recent research suggests it may give a voice to women otherwise unable to voice public complaints.

As we have seen, the involvement of European merchants in the cloth trade in Africa goes back many centuries to the first explorations of the West African coast by Portuguese navigators. Although these traders found Africa to be a ready market for almost all forms of cloth they also rapidly discovered that their African customers had clear and firmly expressed tastes and rejected any novel imports which did not satisfy their requirements in terms of quality and design. Trading company records from the seventeenth century list for the advice of ships' captains the types of cloth suitable for sale in Africa. Attempts by European manufacturers to tailor their output to meet these tastes date back at least to the eighteenth century when Manchester factories produced vast quantities of imitation Indian Madras cloths, displacing most of the genuine Indian cloth that traders had previously

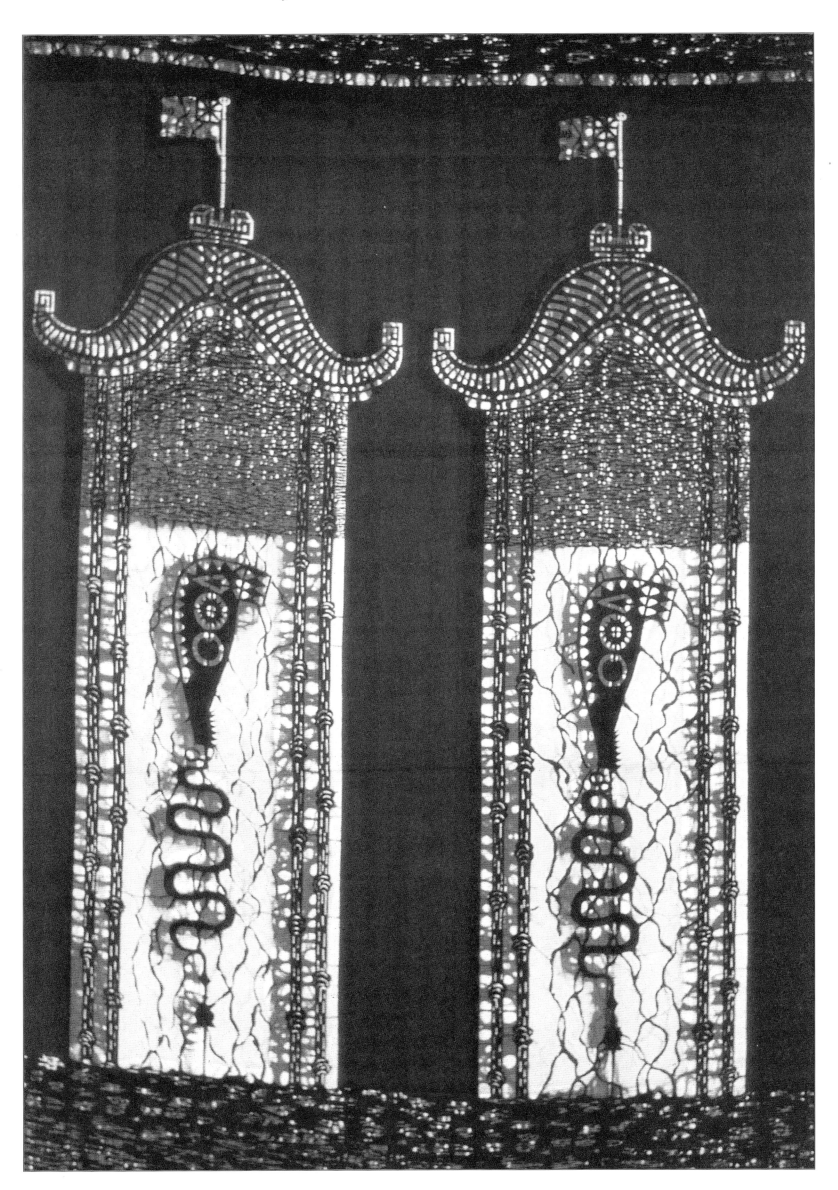

sold in West Africa. The development of African wax cloth began with a similar attempt by European manufacturers to undercut local textile industries in colonised countries, in this case with an effort by Dutch factories to supply machine-made imitations of Javanese batik to its colony in Indonesia. Towards the end of the nineteenth century a Belgian printer, J.B. Previnaire, working in the Dutch town of Haarlem, adapted a French banknote printing machine so that it could apply resin as a resisting agent to both surfaces of cotton cloth. The technique was rapidly modified, with additional areas of color being applied by hand using the wooden blocks as stamps, a technique already in use in both Holland and India to imitate batik. Note that although the cloths are still known as wax resist the actual substance applied to the fabric in order to resist the dye (i.e. protect the covered area while the rest of the cloth is dyed) is a type of resin.

This technique, the details of which we need not go into here, was only partially successful. The resin cracked allowing fine lines of color to penetrate giving a "crackled" effect, and it was found impossible to match up areas of the second color exactly to the first without a slight overlap. But while Indonesian consumers with their long history of batik rejected the imitations, merchants soon discovered there was a ready market in the Dutch trading posts of the Gold Coast (now Ghana). The way had been prepared for this by earlier imports of batik to the region by Dutch merchants, and by cloth brought home by African soldiers recruited by the Dutch for service in Indonesia.

Within a few years factories in Manchester,

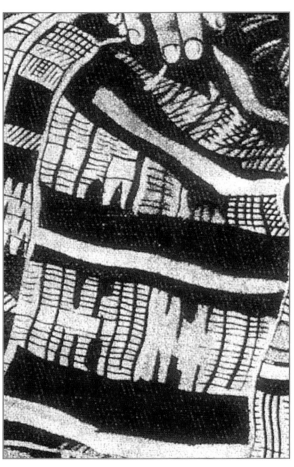

ABOVE (DETAIL) AND RIGHT
Fancy print cotton textile. Dating from October 1929, this cloth was ordered by the United Africa Company to commemorate the Asantehene Nana Premph. It is the earliest known example of a commemorative print.

England were utilising a similar technique, with firms in Switzerland, France, and even Japan, entering the trade in the 1920s and 1930s. The crackling and irregularities perceived as faults in Indonesia were soon regarded as essential features of the cloth style by African consumers and are still carefully replicated in factories today.

Once the cloth was being produced specifically for sale in West Africa, designs began to be adapted to fit them more specifically to local tastes and concerns. A key figure in this process was Ebenezer Brown Flemming, a Glasgow merchant who, until his death in 1912, was involved in supplying designs to both the Haarlem Cotton Company and its rivals in Manchester. While Flemming himself may well not have been to Africa, he was able to draw on close links with market traders in the Gold Coast to initiate numerous designs, many of which remain in production today. The archives kept by the two surviving European producers of wax-print cloth indicate, for example, that in 1904 they were producing a pattern known as "Sword of Kingship" with a design based on the royal swords of the Ashanti king. The same design, showing the spiral-bladed sword, known in Nigeria as "Corkscrew," is widely available throughout Africa in the 1990s.

The designers working for the factories still rely on close contacts with traders throughout Africa, augmented by their records of past successes and failures, to form a detailed picture of variations in taste and preference for certain colors and designs throughout all the regions of Africa in which their cloths are sold. It is common, for example, for the same design to be printed in different colors for Ghana, Nigeria, and Zaire.

The next major development was the introduction of various types of direct-printing technology to produce cheaper imitations of wax prints. These cloths, generally known as "fancy prints," can be easily distinguished since the design appears only on the top surface of the cloth. The technology has one advantage over resin-resist printing, however, in that it allows finer detail of design, and particularly the reproduction of photographs on the cloth. Since the late 1920s these advantages have assisted in the popularity of the cloths as a means of commemorating individuals and events. Since the independence era of the 1960s most African countries have set up their own textile industries, drawing on the technology and design repertoire of the European firms. Assisted by protective tariffs and lower labor costs, they have undercut their overseas rivals and driven most of them from the business. In the mid-1990s only two firms, Vlisco based in Helmond in the Netherlands and A. Brunnschweiler & Company of Hyde near Manchester, still compete with the local producers such as Afprint of Lagos, Akosombo Textiles of Ghana, Sotiba of Senegal, and numerous other firms throughout sub-Saharan Africa. In Nigeria, for example, Dutch and English wax cloths are now prestige items, costing up to three times as much as the local output. Local firms initiate some of their own designs and there is a lively and often acrimonious debate over the ownership of copyrights — somewhat ironic given the origins of the industry.

Although the early years of the trade reveal some design directions that were not often subsequently pursued, such as imagery from ancient Egypt, the main features of wax cloth design set down in the first decades of the century still guide most of the hundreds of new versions that are manufactured each year. John Picton, who is currently working on a history of the industry, has noted that the vast majority of designs may be categorised into one of five groups. Firstly

Wax print cotton textile printed in Manchester, England, in 1961 to mark the opening of the Guinness factory in Lagos.

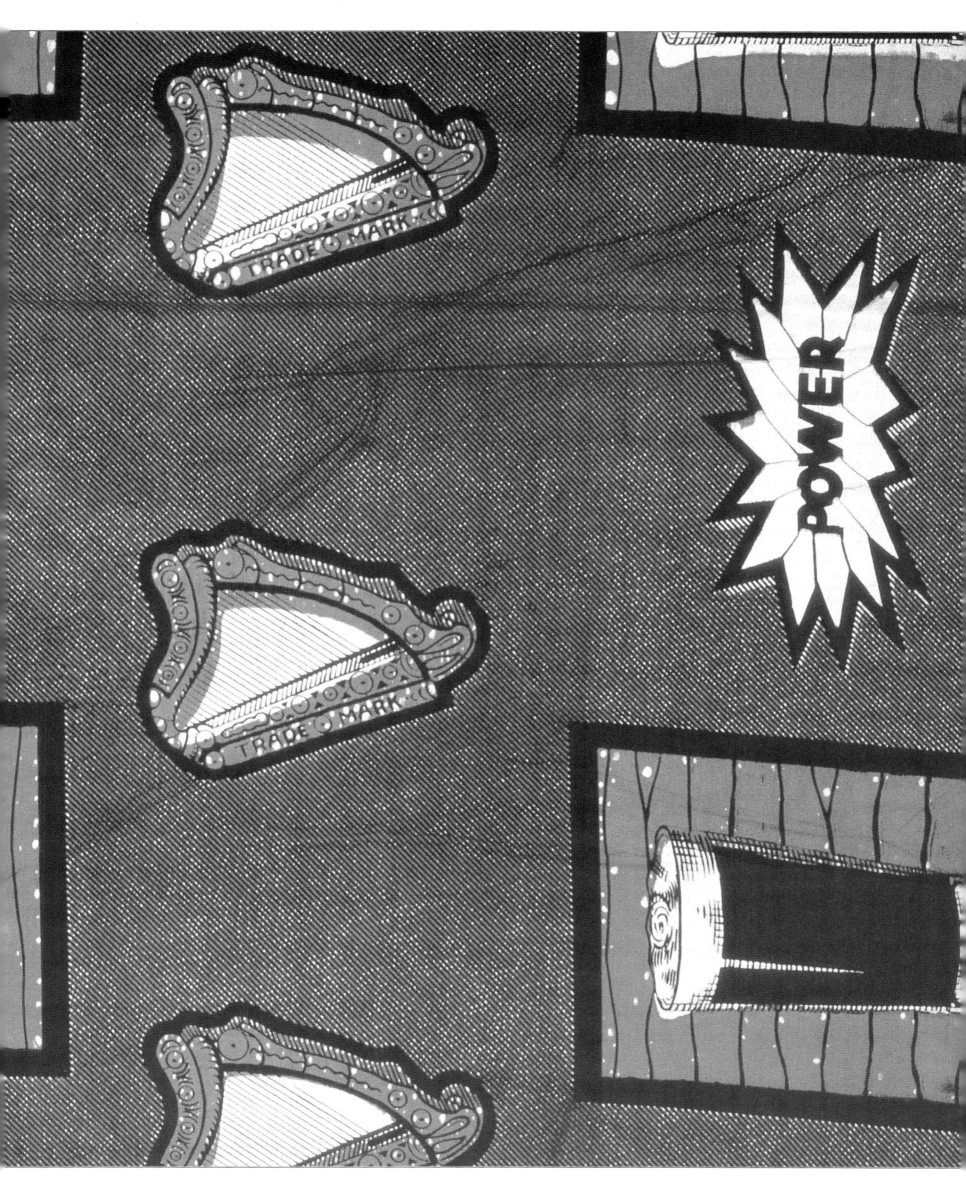

there are still numerous patterns which reflect the influence of Indonesian batik designs such as complex floral and bird motifs and the tail feathers of the sacred bird Garuda, a design known in West Africa as "bunch of bananas." Then there are designs that draw on the well-known Ashanti interest in proverbs, either directly through the incorporation of a written proverb on the cloth, or more commonly by depicting images that refer to aspects of a proverb. A popular example of this type is a cloth showing a fallen tree in a wood, recalling the Akan proverb "One tree alone cannot stand in the wind," while another combines images of a family with skulls and the warning "Death spoils the family." The design of a spider in its web, popular in Ghana, refers to the Anansi, the spider trickster who is the leading character in many folktales. A third group has designs based on the reproduction of local emblems, usually relating to traditions of kingship or the authority of chieftains such as the ivory mask of the queen mother from Benin. Another example is the "Sword of Kingship" we have already mentioned, which is reinterpreted as a corkscrew in countries where the emblem is not known. A sub-group in this category is the imitation of local forms of hand-woven or hand-decorated textiles, especially of the kente cloth and adinkra of the Ashanti. Designs which have an educational significance are also enduringly popular. One of these is the so-called "Hand and Fingers" design, which was in production by at least 1905 and has continued through numerous modifications ever since. This design, which shows the palm of a hand surrounded by rows of fingers, has many levels of symbolism: it refers to a proverb likening the interdependence of ruler and ruled to the hand and its fingers; the educational element comes from the twelve pennies in the palm making up one shilling; while it also recalls the "Hand of Fatima" a popular Islamic emblem for warding off the evil eye. The "Alphabet" design popular for many decades is an even more explicit example of this didactic group. The fifth group is the commemorative cloths depicting individual and events. To this list we can add a sixth group which features once novel items of modern technology incorporated

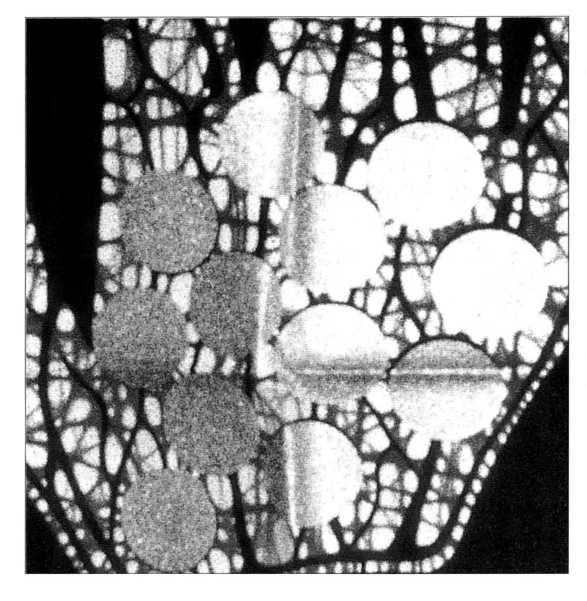

LEFT (DETAIL) AND RIGHT
Wax print cotton textile. One of the latest (1990) English versions of the long-running "Hands and Fingers" design.

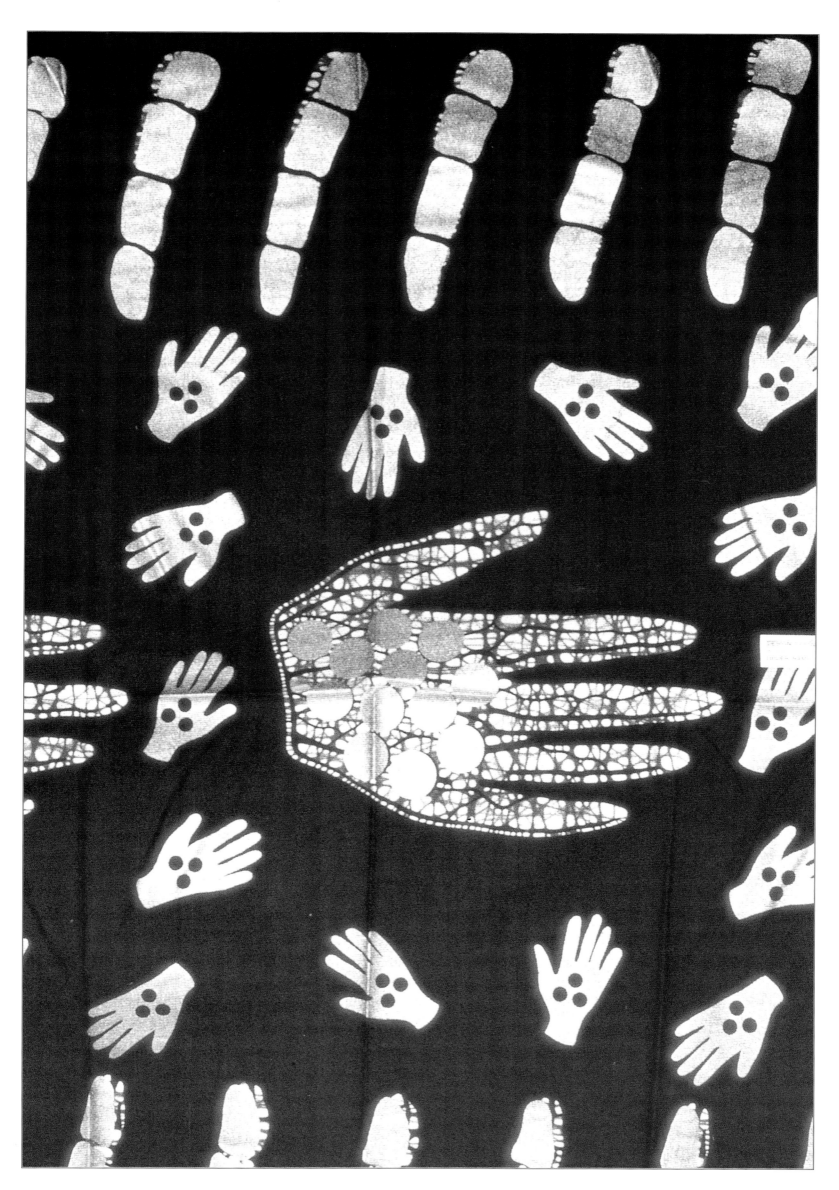

into African life in the twentieth century — records, cars and motorbikes, the popular "Cutlery Set" design, even mini-skirts.

We have seen in previous chapters that many African peoples have long used cloths as a way of demonstrating group unity at a variety of important social events, using customs such as the aso ebi of the Yoruba. Commemorative cloths draw on traditions of this type to provide a means by which organisations, governments, and wealthy individuals can promote themselves or their interests. Cloth printed with portraits was first commissioned in the late 1920s for funerals of figures such as the Ashanti king, but was quickly adopted to commemorate a wider range of events. The cloth could be sold cheaply or even given away to followers or party supporters, producing a large gathering of people who were visibly expressing their apparent support for an individual or cause. The political leaders of independent Africa were quick to realise the potential of cloth as a medium for harnessing support, and whether for election campaigns or more general expressions of national solidarity, virtually all of them from Sekou Toure to Nelson Mandela have been depicted on cloths. Governments also commissioned cloths to promote campaigns relating to issues such as health or literacy, or to record events such as the Festival of Black Arts and Culture in Lagos. Other organisations followed suit, from the Catholic church marking papal visits to banks advertising their centenary in business. The relatively low cost of local fancy printing meant that wealthy families could also remember a departed grandfather or mother by wearing a cloth bearing his or her portrait at the funeral ceremonies. In Nigeria a variant form of this developed in the 1940s and 1950s when velvet cloths were ordered from England imprinted with photographs and proverbs for use as a luxury version at funerals. Other cloths were produced without commission by textile manufacturers hoping to cash in on an interest in popular sporting figures such as Muhammad Ali or events such as the World Cup.

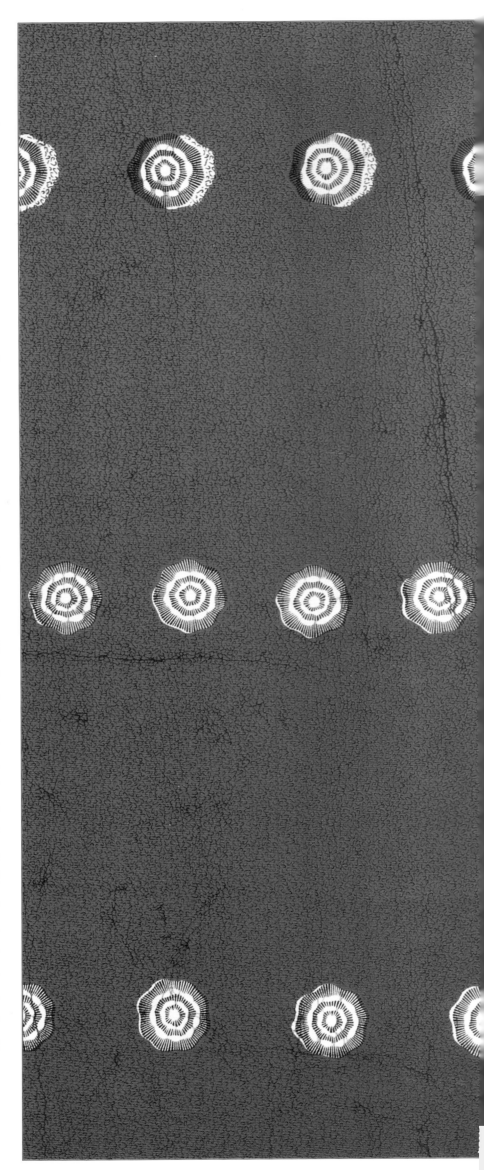

RIGHT
Wax print cotton textile, "Record" design,
A. Brunnschweiler & Co, England, 1990s.

120

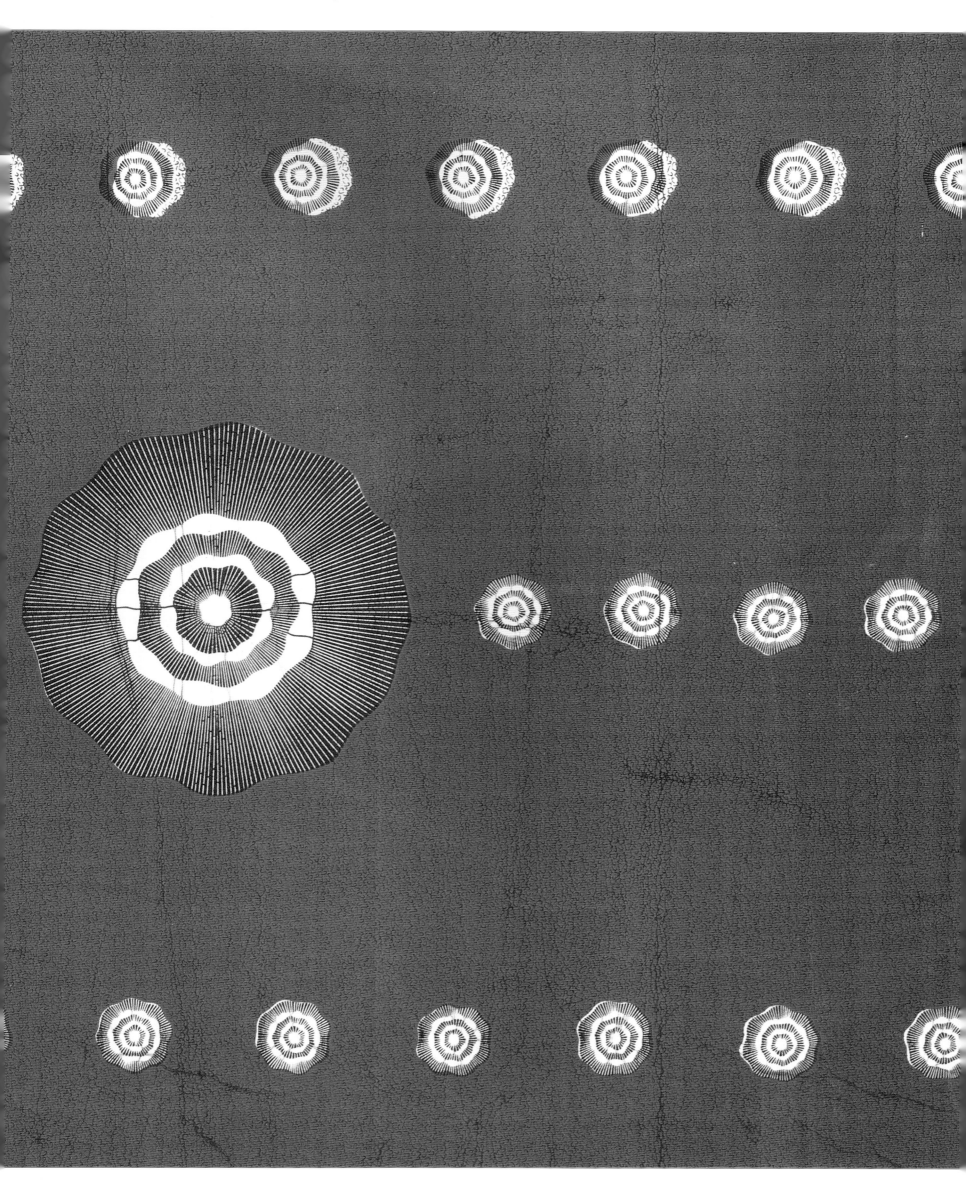

Another dimension of the communicative potential of wax cloths is far removed from the commemorative designs that promote the wealthy and powerful. In the last few years several researchers have noted that women have been able to use the imagery and associated proverbs of some wax-print cloths to send messages they would otherwise be unable to express publicly. As yet it is unclear how widespread this practice may be but it certainly adds a new dimension to some familiar designs. Susan Domowitz noted that among the Anyi of Côte D'Ivoire the tensions underlying the apparent harmony of a polygamous household were expressed by a cloth featuring circular designs. The cloth was known as "co-wife rivalry is like cow dung," a proverb that ends "the top is dry but the inside is sticky." The familiar spider designs are associated with the warning proverb "what one does to the small harmless spider , one does not do to the big dangerous one." A woman who was tired of her husband's unfaithfulness could let him know by wearing a cloth featuring a bird flying from the open door of a cage. The name of this design is "You go out, I go out"! Another one bears the equally blunt title "condolences to my husband's mistress."

African wax-printed cloth, is then far more than just a colorful and exotic mode of dress. Its history is bound up with the complex interconnections fostered by the colonial involvement in Africa and the subsequent efforts of African nations to regain control over their economic destiny. Its design repertoire blends contemporary African concerns with imagery drawn from this historical legacy. Its accessibility lends itself to both commemoration of the powerful and personal critique by the poor. It provides both everyday dress and a raw material for exclusive designers. It reproduces traditional fabric designs but also celebrates the novel and remarkable. As such it is a fitting note on which to conclude this introduction to the diversity of African textile artistry.

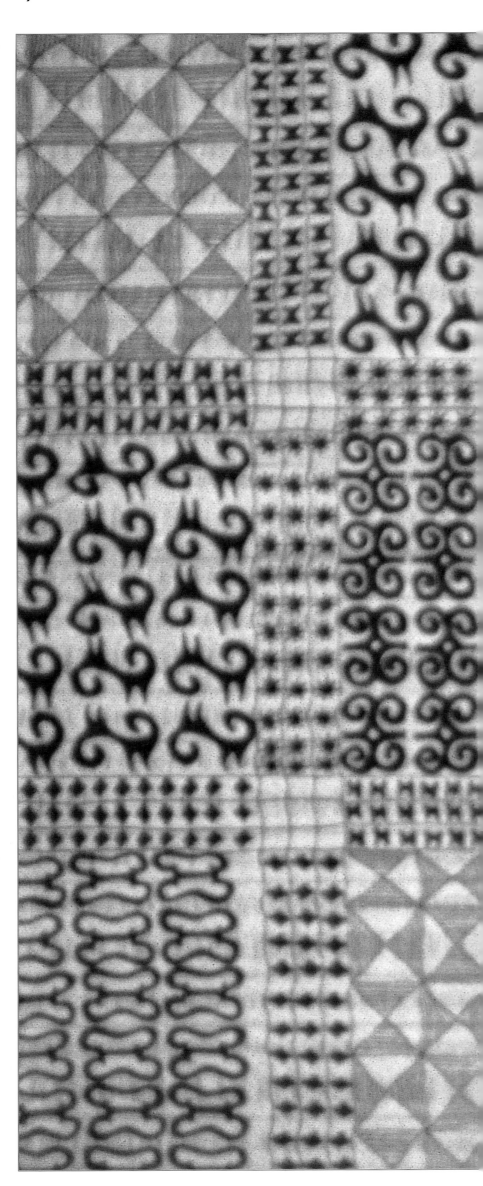

RIGHT
Wax print cotton textile, "Adinkra" design on "seersucker" fabric; Vlisco, Netherlands, 1990s.

LEFT
Woman wearing the design Owu Se Fie, "Death spoils the family,"
popular in Ghana with people in mourning; 1994.

ABOVE
Wax print cotton textile. Contemporary Ghanaian version
of the long established "Alphabet" design.

*Fancy print cotton textile. A variant of
the popular "Spider" design, with other
motifs including the "mat" and "record."
Ghana, 1990s.*

Wax print cotton textile, printed on a
patterned brocade fabric.
A. Brunnschweiler & Co,
England, 1990s.

CREDITS

The Author and Publisher graterfully acknowledge the assistance provided by those lent photographs andtextiles for use in this book as acknowledged in the list of page credits below. In particular we'd like to thank Simon Clay for his studio photography and Peter Adler for all the textiles he provided.

Author's Collection
1, 3, 5, 6/7, 24/5, 28, 33, 34(both), 35, 36/7, 40, 41, 42, 43, 44(top), 45, 91, 100, 101, 103, 104, 105, 106(top), 107, 108, 109, 120/1, 126

Author's photograph
10/11, 15, 16, 17, 74/5, 94, 95, 96/7, 98, 99, 102, 110/1, 122/3, 125, 127

Courtesy Ministry of Information, Oyo State, Ibadan
2, 18, 19, 20/1, 22

Werner Foreman Archive
8, 9 (Petrie Museum, University College, London), 64, 68, 69

Dr James Bynon
12, 13

Dr John Picton
23, 65, 66, 112, 113, 116/7, 118, 119, 124

via Dr John Picton
114, 115

Peter Adler Gallery, London
26, 27, 30, 31, 32, 38(both), 39(both), 44(bottom), 46, 47, 49, 50, 51, 52, 53, 54, 55, 56, 57, 58, 59, 60, 61(both), 62/3(both), 67, 70, 71, 72/3, 76, 77, 78, 79, 80/1, 82, 83, 84(both), 85, 86, 87, 89(both), 90, 106(bottom)

African Escape
92/3, 93(top)

FURTHER READING

JOHN PICTON & JOHN MACK, AFRICAN TEXTILES, BRITISH MUSEUM PUBLICATIONS, LONDON (1989 2ND EDITION)

CLAIRE POLAKOFF, AFRICAN TEXTILES AND DYEING TECHNIQUES, ROUTLEDGE & KEGAN PAUL (1982)

ELISHA P. RENNE, CLOTH THAT DOES NOT DIE, UNIVERSITY OF WASHINGTON PRESS (1995)

ROY SIEBER, AFRICAN TEXTILES AND DECORATIVE ARTS, MUSEUM OF MODERN ART, NEW YORK (1972)

CHRISTOPHER SPRING & JULIE HUDSON, NORTH AFRICAN TEXTILES, BRITISH MUSEUM PUBLICATIONS, LONDON (1995)